The **MG** Story

The MG Story

THE STORY OF EVERY M.G.
FROM "OLD NO. 1" IN 1923 TO THE
MOST MODERN, WITH SPECIFICATIONS
AND PHOTOS

by

JOSEPH H. WHERRY

Chilton's Sebring Series

CHILTON BOOKS

A DIVISION OF CHILTON COMPANY
Publishers
Philadelphia   New York

To Carol, my daughter

Foreword

WE consider it natural today to have on any given weekend somewhere in the United States either an important Sports Car Race or Rallye or some form of Concours d'Elegance. No one is surprised to see our streets and highways enlivened by sleek sports cars of both domestic and foreign origin.

But it was not always so. The popularity of sports cars began to grow here only a little more than twenty years ago. I am convinced that the little MG-TC, which made its appearance on our shores after World War II, was a big factor in accelerating the interest of American motorists in sports cars—an interest that grew and grew in spite of the dour predictions of the leaders of the U.S. automobile industry to the contrary, leaders who held fast to the myth that women buy the cars and men have lost their love of tinkering with engines and driving for its own sake.

The stark, spindly, 19-inch wire wheels and the 4-speed transmission of the MG-TC were a revelation to the young who had never driven a Stutz or a Mercer, and a nostalgic reminder to the older ones who had.

It is most gratifying to see the history of this make so thoroughly compiled and documented and its racing exploits so well recorded in this book by Mr. Wherry. He has done a superb job and deserves from all of us MG owners and fanciers three rousing cheers.

ALEC ULMANN
President
Automobile Racing Club of Florida, Inc.

Acknowledgments

THE Author wishes to express his sincere thanks to the many people who have cooperated so kindly: The M.G. Car Company, and the British Motor Corporation in the United Kingdom and in the United States; Mr. Al Arth of British Motor Cars, Inc., of San Francisco; Mr. Ed Fitzpatrick of Santa Rosa British Cars, Santa Rosa, California; Mr. John Duncan and Miss Helen F. Leech, president and vice-president respectively of the Northern California chapter of the M.G. Owners Club; Mr. William F. McCormick, Jr., manager of the San Francisco Region of the Sports Car Club of America; the Editors of *The Autocar;* and the Editors of *The Motor.* Very special thanks to David and Debby Anne who missed many swimming jaunts during the summer when this book was being written; and to Bettye, my wife, without whose typing and proofreading the under-signed would have been swamped. Finally, thanks to all M.G. enthusiasts for just being.

JOSEPH H. WHERRY

Contents

Specifications appear at ends of chapters.

List of Illustrations

The MG Story

1 Out of the Morris Garages

IN mid-March, 1923, Cecil Kimber, the astonishingly ingenious general manager of a garage firm in Oxford, England, began the construction of a lean two-seater that was destined to foreshadow a long line of sports cars and to bring the joys of motoring for its own sake to a worldwide fraternity. Some accounts have it that Kimber rode his Special in competition in the 1923 London to Land's End Trial and won a gold medal. Although Kimber drove a Special sporting type in the 1923 event, it was *not* an M.G. in the strict sense of the marque's name.

The genesis of the M.G. is somewhat confusing, particularly because the Special that Kimber built in 1923 is officially M.G. No. 1. The confusion is scarcely dispelled by the plaque, gracing the restored speedster,

"Old No. 1," the first M.G., was all muscle. Built in March, 1923, it later won a gold medal in its first competitive effort driven by its creator, Cecil Kimber. (M.G. Car Co. Ltd.)

which identifies the year as 1925. There are valid reasons, however, for the mix-up in the genealogy of the marque though one must admit that the logic is not always apparent.

To add to the reader's curiosity, the Special built in 1923 won in 1925 the *first* gold medal ever awarded to an M.G. Although the red two-seater was the *first* M.G., and "the start of it all," as the works managing director, John Thornley, put it in his excellent *Maintaining the Breed,* the M.G. as a marque in its own right was officially established and advertised in the motoring press in the early spring of 1924. Consequently, enthusiasm for the *marque* M.G. is well based upon more than four decades of "Safety Fast" achievements.

The intriguing background of this long line of sports cars began in 1893, when William Richard Morris, just fifteen years old, took a job in a bicycle shop in Oxford at 5 shillings a week—about 70 cents today and barely $1.25 then. In less than a year, young Morris went into business for himself in his father's woodshed in nearby Cowley. After making a bit of a local name for himself repairing bicycles, Morris purchased parts and assembled the first Morris bicycle before the end of 1894. Soon he rented sales and repair space at 48 High Street in Oxford, the first garage to bear his name. Business boomed and around 1901 Morris machined purchased castings, built an engine, and turned out his first motorcycle.

By 1908, Morris had been through several business

adventures including a partnership or two, had come under the spell of the automobile, and was sole owner of The Oxford Garage. This establishment was registered in 1910 as "The Morris Garage" and here Morris, now in his early thirties, repaired cars and motorcycles of a score of makes. He was also the agent for a number of new cars including the Hupmobile, probably the only American car he ever sold. By 1913, Morris had two more establishments including the old Queens Hotel in Oxford. This became his new car showroom and the business was re-registered to accommodate the plural locations as "The Morris Garages, W. R. Morris, Proprietor."

Even in 1910, Morris was enjoying increasing prosperity as a new car dealer. Like others in the boom years of the motor car prior to World War I, Morris began investigating the possibility of making his own cars. In 1912, with the assurance of backing by the Earl of Macclesfield, Morris registered "W. R. M. Motors Limited" and began to design his first car.

In those days, scores of makes utilized engines, transmissions, chassis frames, suspension and other parts which were turned out to the specifications of the many manufacturer-assemblers by specialist firms. But whereas the majority of car makers sought to keep secret the names of their component manufacturers, Morris took a different approach. He reasoned that quantity production would be essential if success was the object, and he further determined—and wisely as matters developed—that he would forthrightly proclaim to the public that his vehicles, though of his own design, employed major components from suppliers with already established reputations.

Finally, after many frustrations, Morris introduced his first car, the Morris Oxford, about the middle of 1913. The wheelbase was 84 inches, the tread 40 inches, and the suspension by half-elliptic leaf springs in front and by three-quarter elliptics in the rear carrying a worm drive axle. The axles and steering gear were supplied by E. G. Wrigley, Ltd., and the 4-cylinder T-head 60 x 90 mm. engines, 3-speed gearbox, and 36-plate clutches were the products of White & Poppe, Ltd., who also supplied engines for more than a dozen already established makes including the Singer, which had some fame in America after World War II. Morris designed the bodies for the new Oxford and they were coach-built by Raworths, Ltd., of Oxford. Engineering and assembly were done in Cowley, near Oxford, where Morris had purchased old, unused military college buildings.

Stewart and Arden, a respected London automobile sales firm, ordered a batch of four hundred Oxfords and the Morris empire was on its way.

The tread was soon increased to 42 inches in an attempt to cure steering problems, and the clutch was redesigned with two fewer plates to lessen the tendency to stick in cold weather. The Oxford quickly established a reputation for dependability and speed. *The Cyclecar* of August 6, 1913, reported that first gear would take it to 20 mph plus, second cog was good for

Bloodline ancestor of the first M.G. was the 1913 "Bullnose" Morris Oxford, the first car built by the late Viscount Nuffield. (British Motor Corp.)

over 38 mph, and maximum speed for a shade over 50 mph.

With a quickly arranged network of distributors, the Oxford quickly caught on and did well in sporting events in 1913. In the London to Edinburgh to London Trial, a spanking new Oxford was awarded a gold medal; in the Dutch Reliability Trials, a six-day affair, an Oxford took first place; and Oxfords took the top three places in the Oxfordshire Motor Club's annual hill climb. In all, 393 cars were produced in 1913, all with the famous "bullnose" radiator shell that was to be retained well into the M.G. age. By the time the 1914–1918 war erupted, the Oxford's tread had been increased to 45 inches, more body styles added to the line including a sporty torpedo, and an enclosed torque tube final drive featured.

Meanwhile, the Morris Garages, the original and affiliated enterprise, went from strength to strength in the selling and repairing of cars, mostly Morrises. By the end of 1923 some 35,000 Morris Oxfords and Cowleys (a lower priced variant) had been produced. The White & Poppe engines plus others, including Hotchkiss, and Continental Red Seal engines from the U.S.A., were rapidly giving way to engines made by Morris.

At this time, the Morris Garages, though owned by W. R. Morris, were operating independently. Cecil Kimber, a motorcycle racer, had come to the attention of Morris during a business visit by the latter to E. G. Wrigley Ltd. in 1921. Soon Kimber joined the staff of The Morris Garages and in mid-1922 became the general manager. He set to work developing a Morris Cowley Chummy two-seater powered by a 1,548 cc. Hotchkiss engine.

The Chummy was a 102-inch-wheelbase Morris chassis fitted with lightweight, sporting, two-seater coachwork by either Carbodies of Coventry or Raworths of Oxford. The Chummy Specials were products of The Morris Garages who "bought in" the chassis from W. R. M. Motors. In a sense, these Chummy rigs, with the scantiest of fenders and a minimum of frills, were the first Morris Garages, or M.G., cars. During late 1921 through 1923 Kimber was making The Garages famous with a steady but limited production.

It was with one of these machines that Kimber won a gold medal for a perfect performance in the 1923 London to Land's End Trial, and at about this time he must have begun the construction of the M.G. No. 1 mentioned earlier.

A spartan vehicle it was and is, for Old No. 1 now has an honored place in the British Motor Corporation's museum. No. 1 was a Morris chassis stripped of all unnecessary items. The "innards" of the 1,548 cc. Hotchkiss engine were polished, the pistons and rods balanced, and a single S.U. carburetor with leather bellows fitted. (S.U. stands for Skinners Union, a firm founded in 1910 and purchased by Morris in 1926.) Kimber retained the distinctive "bullnose" radiator shell, added a feather-light, boattail, two-seater body with staggered seats to reduce width and weight, employed just a hint of mudguards, and fitted 9-inch

The first M.G. seen from the traffic side. Note the external handbrake and bare minimum of body. (British Motor Corp.)

drum brakes on all four wheels. The latter were wire-spoked and secured at the hubs with only three bolts each. For further security he installed an external hand-brake, a pair of small cowl lamps, and a single head-light. Instrumentation was a tachometer, speedometer, ammeter, and a fuel-air and oil pressure gauge. Springs were snubbed down and the payoff was a precise-handling road-course machine capable of better than 80 mph.

Reportedly, Old No. 1 actually carried the M.G.'s distinctive octagonal marker when Cecil Kimber produced this speedster. With this car, Kimber was the sensation of the 1925 London-Land's End Trial in which he won a gold medal for perfect performance. Someone subsequently bought this M.G. Special and it was lost through a series of sales until rescued in more recent years from a Manchester junk heap, returned to the factory, and given a thorough restoration.

But despite the facts about this car, the history of the earliest generations of the M.G. is often in dispute. Most information indicates that No. 1 was completed in late 1923 but not entered in the London-Land's End Trial by Kimber until 1925 as described above. The museum badge on the restored car's front says both "No. 1" and "1925" so the only logical conclusion is that it was built in 1923, functioned as an inspiring prototype to whet the appetites of customers, and then scored its *first and only* competition victory in 1925. These facts make Old No. 1 *the first* M.G., but just barely, as we shall see, for advertisements in the popular press early in 1924 spoke of "The M.G. [in large letters enclosed by an octagon] Super Sports Morris." In this line quoted from a Morris Garages advertisement in the May 1924 *Morris Owner* magazine, the "M.G." is the key to the historical part of the name.

About the time Old No. 1 emerged from the shops of The Morris Garages in Oxford, Kimber and his men designed a lightweight, sporting, roadster body and ordered six of them from Raworths, the coachbuilders. Simultaneously, six Cowley chassis were bought in from the parent W. R. M. Motors. The production Cowley tourer's specifications in brief were: wheelbase, 102 inches; tread (by this date wisely increased), 48 inches; engine, four cylinders, cast-in-block, three main bearings, 1,548 cc. displacement, R.A.C. rating of 11.9 horsepower. The frame was 24 inches wide, 9-inch-diameter drum brakes were on all four wheels, the transmission was 3-speed and the propeller shaft was inclosed in a torque tube.

In addition to the coachwork, Kimber's magic included modified steering which raked the column downward to clear the lowered dashboard, a special 30 mm. Solex carburetor, redesigned springs with decreased camber and special shock absorbers, switching the handbrake to the right side, and somewhat quicker gear ratios although the precise changes here are not definitely known. "Special tuning" of the engine was claimed, the details of which are obscure, although balancing of the rods and pistons is understood to have

The first production series of M.G. cars was based upon the chassis of Morris Oxford and Cowley cars. Shown is the 1923 Cowley. (*The Motor*)

been done. A Smiths 80 mph speedometer was fitted, but it is doubted that these M.G. Super Sports Morris cars would go faster than 60 or 65 mph.

However, it is certain that this first series of six production M.G. cars was hand built; that they carried the octagonal emblem, and that they were fine value in 1924, delivering at a moderate price, for the times, of 350 pounds.

Almost immediately, Oxford chassis were ordered by The Morris Garages to fill orders for Specials with four-seater aluminum coachwork of M.G. design but coachbuilt by Carbodies of Coventry. This series—actually a second series—was marketed as the 14/28 M.G. from early in 1924 until well into 1927. The engine was basically the 13.9 h.p. (R.A.C.) Oxford engine of 1,802 cc. displacement. In all, approximately four hundred were built with the four-seat tourer the most popular body style. There were two-seat, boattailed roadsters and four-passenger "Salonette" models, some of the latter having a rear luggage boot.

Polished aluminum paneling covered the coach-type, seasoned hardwood frame. Even the hood (or "bonnet") was aluminum. Only the famous "bullnose" radiator shell, which had been a Morris hallmark since the first Oxford in 1913, betrayed the basic parentage. The windshield, usually a three-piece affair, was sharply slanted; louvers in the hood facilitated engine cooling; and it is said that the top (or "hood") could be raised and secured without leaving the car. Upholstery was leather dyed in blue or claret and the gracefully shaped

A fine car at a moderate price was the 1924–1927 M.G. 14/28 sports tourer with the bullnose radiator shell. (M.G. Car Co. Ltd.)

Louvres atop the bonnet and polished aluminum coachwork made the Type 14/28 a sparkling beauty. (British Motor Corp.)

fenders were painted to match. The 3-bolt wheels were either artillery spoked or of Dunlop wire over which Ace aluminum discs were fitted.

These were sporty machines, but improvements were continually being made. By 1925, the wheelbase was extended 6 inches, 12-inch brakes were fitted and a vacuum servo was added to handle the brisker perform-ance. The radiator core was enlarged, exterior door handles were fitted, and the upper part of the bodies was painted to match the fenders. In a way, these changes constituted a new series. By 1926, a calorimeter replaced the Boyce Moto Meter and the headlights had a Barker dipping device which tilted both lamps.

The 14/28 M.G. won its share of trials and fame; and a few found their way into foreign lands by way of royal purchasers. The first foreign recorded racing victory by an M.G. was in Argentina in 1927. By this time the familiar "bullnose" radiator shell had been phased out by the parent Morris factory and replaced by a rather uninspired flat shell.

In mid-1926, Morris Motors ceased to be a private company and issued stock. However, The Morris Ga-rages and several other firms remained independent and continued wholly owned by W. R. Morris.

Due to the three variations on the original Cowley-through-Oxford-modifications theme, it appeared to The Morris Garages that some means to identify model series was overdue. Consequently, after a few of the flat-nosed 14/28 models were produced, the 1927 series was named the 14/40 Mark IV, and was advertised

The aluminum-sheathed coachwork of the Type 14/40 Mark IV was finished with an engine-turned motif on some models as on this two-seater sports model. (British Motor Corp.)

Coachwork by Carbodies of Coventry distinguished many of the Type 14/40 Mark IV roadsters like this one with the distinctive rear deck. (British Motor Corp.)

as delivering 35 bhp at 4,000 rpm. In the next two years, about 700 Mark IVs were built in a variety of body styles with performance topping out at about 70 mph.

While The Morris Garages continued to sell the 14/40 Mark IV as rapidly as they could modify Oxford chassis and obtain coachwork for installation, Cecil Kimber continued to look for ways to further magnify M.G. cars as a marque in their own right.

Speed with safety plus magnificence had already proven to be a valid formula and when W. R. M. Motors developed a 2½-liter, overhead camshaft, 6-cylinder engine for the Morris line, Kimber knew he had the nucleus for an M.G. to suit the most discriminating buyer. In August, 1928, the M.G. models designation system took another turn which still tends to confuse enthusiasts today: the first 18/80 Mark I rolled from The Morris Garages while the 14/40 Mark IV was still being produced!

To make the recording and dating of M.G. types even more amazing, Kimber and his two chief assistants, the late George King and Cecil Cousins, were also designing the first of the fabulous M.G. Midgets, the type M. This and the rest of the Midget tribe will be discussed later.

In 1928 and 1929, The Morris Garages were humming with the production of M.G. Six 18/80 Mark I cars. Making the beehive a virtual madhouse, production was moved from the Garages to the Pavlova works in Abingdon in September, 1929, and the M.G. Car

The 14/40 Mark IV Tourer was a prestige car for families with a sporting bent. (British Motor Corp.)

The Type Six 18/80 Mark I was fitted with various kinds of coachwork and had a 2½-litre 6-cylinder engine. (British Motor Corp.)

Company Ltd. was organized with Cecil Kimber as managing director under the corporate umbrella of Morris, who was now Sir William.

The new car was distinguished on several counts: it was the *first* 6-cylinder M.G. produced in a series (hence the logic of Mark I designation), *first* with an M.G. chassis frame and suspension that owed nothing to the related Morris cars, *first* with an overhead camshaft, *first* with center-locking wire wheels, *first* with strictly M.G. styling including the narrowly tapered, vertical radiator shell that hallmarked the entire M.G. line through 1953, and *first* developed from absolute scratch as a sports car.

The 18/80 Mark I was also the *first* M.G. to enter the higher-priced field since prices began at 520 pounds which was by no means cheap, a pound sterling then being worth close to five dollars. Body styles, all coach-built, ran the gamut from fabric-covered tourers to aluminum-bodied roadsters with rumble ("dicky") seats, and saloons. It was a man's car in every sporting respect, as the specifications chart accompanying this chapter shows. The Six 18/80 Mark I still had a three-speed gearbox, but it developed approximately 80 bhp and its ohc, long-stroke engine (69 x 110 mm.) was smooth as silk, genuinely providing the advertised 8 to 80 mph in top gear. Big on its 114-inch wheelbase and weighing upwards of 2,600 pounds at the curb, this car had, unfortunately, a reputation for skidding. Nevertheless, the Mark I actually provided the impetus that launched M.G. into racing.

Note the full bucket seats in this Type 18/80 Mark I two-seater. The Mark II looked the same but had different specifications. (British Motor Corp.)

While the lovely 18/80 Mark I was selling briskly (as it would until July, 1931), Kimber completely redesigned the chassis, beefing it up by more than 300 pounds and increasing the tread from 48 inches to 52 inches front and rear, the wheelbase remaining the same. The 18/80 Mark II had 14-inch drums instead of the Mark I's 12-inch drums, and enthusiasts would have a fly-off handbrake. There was automatic Tecalemit chassis lubrication, and best of all, a new 4-speed crash type gearbox. The 2,468 cc. engine, with its single chain-driven, overhead camshaft, Lucas ignition, dual 1¼-inch horizontal S.U. carburetors (Morris had purchased this firm a year or two previously) and full sports type instrumentation, remained. Though weighing, with coachwork, upward of 3,000 pounds, and costing from 625 pounds up, the better-geared 18/80 Mark II is said to have been able to top a true 80 mph. Superb road machines, one a Mark II saloon, made a perfect run in the 1930 Monte Carlo Rally.

Some 750 of these closely related luxury Sixes were built and sold up to October, 1932. To identify this car more closely for those who seek model identification, the 18/80 Mark II was also known as Type A.

While the 18/80 Marks I and II were joining the ranks of the large luxury sporting machines, Kimber was creating one of his most talked about cars, short-lived though it was, the beautiful Six 18/100 Mark III. This road-racing, International Class, open four-seater sports car was also known as "Tigress" and, alas, as the Type B. Weighing in at about 3,100 pounds, the "Tigress" had an extensively modified engine based

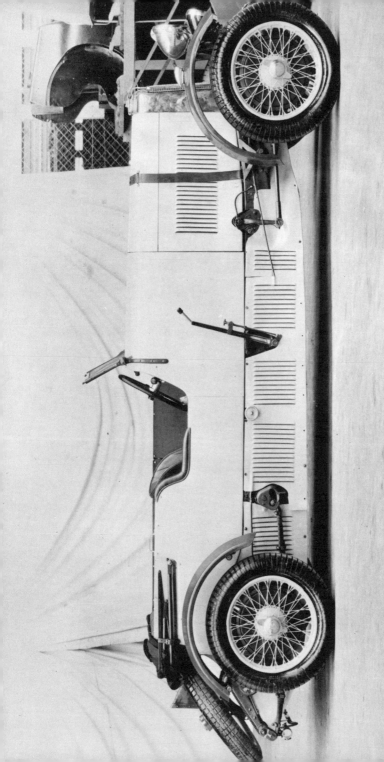

The very rare M.G. Type 18/100 Mark III Tigress, a special 6-cylinder racing machine, had a career as brief at it was colorful. (M.G. Car Co. Ltd.)

A wonderful sight to meet head on—the 18/100 Mark III Tigress—a business-like machine. (British Motor Corp. of Canada Ltd.)

on the 18/80 Mark I/II and cost a fancy 895 pounds or about $8,400 in today's inflated money. Only five were built during 1930–1931. The Tigress was a magnificent, "hairy" vehicle destined to a too brief career in racing, the purpose for which it was made.

The Six 18/100 Mark III was based on the 18/80 Mark II chassis with modifications that included a polished steering mechanism with a longer drop arm, a special 28-gallon fuel tank beneath the floor in front of the rear axle, a brake-adjusting mechanism within the driver's reach, double Hartford shock absorbers (eight in all), and 19-inch knock-off wire wheels. The engine had a new dual ignition head with inclined valves, and inlet ports in the head (the 18/80 Mark I/II ports were in the block); and its compression ratio was increased from 5.8 to 6.9 to 1. Lubrication system changes included a dry sump with the 4½-gallon oil tank and dual oil pumps mounted out front. A specially-made pair of S.U. downdraft carburetors and carefully balanced crankshaft and rods developed approximately 100 bhp, and a maximum speed of around 100 mph must have been rather easily attained, for the engine is said to have turned in excess of 5,000 rpm. Supporting this, the factory listed as the capacity of the 4.27 to 1 rear axle a speed of 20.4 mph per 1,000 rpm.

This machine, with its Brooklands exhaust doubtless terrifying the non-sporting types, was entered by its builders in the Junior Car Club's Double Twelve Hour Race at Brooklands in May, 1930. After two hours of lapping at around 86 mph, letting the familiar Bentleys, Lagondas, and others see its form, one of the S.U.'s came apart and tore up the rocker gear.

The mighty Mark III Tigress was never again entered in competition by the factory. However, the new M.G. Car Company Ltd. of Abingdon had arrived in racing, for three new upstart Midgets, Type M, swept the team prize and established a new concept which influenced all engineering and production for nearly a decade. It established M.G. as a marque to contend with wherever motor racing was enjoyed.

SPECIFICATIONS

Type and Name	Cylinders	Bore and Stroke (mm.)	Displacement (cc.)	Compression Ratio (1/m to 1)	Supercharged	Brake Horsepower @ rpm	Transmission Speeds	Gear Ratios and Alternates (if any)	Rear Axle Ratios and Alternates (if any)	Tires	Wheelbase (inches)	Tread, Front and Rear
14/28 M.G. Morris Oxford Super Sports	4	75 x 102	1,802	5.0	no	35 @ 4,000	3	1.00 1.72 3.20	4.42	19 x 4.95 20 x 4.95 (saloon)	102 (1924) 108 (1925	48
14/40 Mark IV (M.G. octagon medallion)	4	75 x 102	1,802	5.0	no	35 @ 4,000	3	1.00 1.72 3.20	4.42	19 x 4.95 20 x 4.95 (saloon)	108	48
18/80 Mark I	6	69 x 110	2,468	5.8	no	not listed (approx. 18 R.A.C.)	3	1.00 1.55 3.10	4.25	19 x 5.00 19 x 4.95	114	48
18/80 Mark II Type A	6	69 x 110	2,468	5.8	no	not listed (approx. 18 R.A.C.)	4	1.00 1.306 2.00 3.42	4.27	19 x 5.00 19 x 4.95	114	52
18/100 Mark III Tigress Type B	6	69 x 110	2,468	6.9	no	not listed (approx. 18 R.A.C.) estimated 95–100 bhp	4	1.00 1.306 1.84 3.42	4.27	19 x 5.00 19 x 4.95	114	52

 The Racers

THE rarest of all the many descendants of Old No. 1 M.G. were the six types built specifically for racing. Of these the abrupt careers of the Six 18/100 Mark III Tigress and the built-to-win-one-event 6-cylinder Type NE are covered elsewhere because their creation was dependent upon the sports car counterparts which preceded them.

Four of the racing types, however, deserve separate examination. These are the C-type "Montlhery," the K3 Magnette, and the Type Q and Type R Midgets, the last being a single seater.

To put the C-type Montlhery Midget racer into proper perspective, a look must first be taken at the one-year existence of the EX120, which first brought Captain George E. T. Eyston into the M.G. orbit and very nearly ended his career.

The EX120 was conceived shortly after the Double Twelve Hour Race at Brooklands in May, 1930, when the M-type Midgets proved themselves capable of far more than had been expected of them. As detailed later in the chapter on *The Mighty Midgets,* the M-type, nevertheless, had certain deficiencies for racing; and consequently a prototype was laid down. This prototype, the EX120, was on a chassis of parallel steel channel rails with tubular cross members. An M-type front axle beam was used. The M's 42-inch tread was virtually the only familiar feature. The frame was swept upward over the front axle and slung beneath the rear where the semi-elliptical springs were fitted through machined slots in the rearmost cross members. Originally, this prototype for the later D-type Midget had an 847 cc. engine. Then it was decided to attack the under-750 cc. Class H records, so the bore was decreased by sleeving to 54 mm. and a special crankshaft decreased the stroke to 81 mm. This modified engine was mounted on three trunnions, in front and on each side. Unblown, this ¾-liter engine developed approximately 44 bhp.

The block and the radiator were bolted rigidly together to eliminate water hose failures due to flexing of the frame during the stress of high-speed testing. Covering all this was a hastily fabricated lightweight aluminum shell with a cockpit opening barely large enough to allow husky George Eyston to insert himself. The shell had a sharply pointed tail and a headrest. A rounded shroud concealed the radiator core.

The bonnet was doubly strapped. The knock-off wire wheels had no mudguards, and the driver had *no* windscreen.

On a bleak November morning with lookouts posted to warn of interference from the authorities, the car achieved 87 mph without reaching maximum speed. J. A. Palms, Eyston, and the crew then packed the EX120 off to the Montlhery track in France for a series of assaults on the under-750 cc. international records. On December 30, 1930, the crew shoe-horned Eyston into the cockpit and the EX120 shattered three international records, taking the 50 Kilometre with 86.38 mph, the 50 Mile at 87.11 mph, and the 100 Kilometre with 87.3 mph.

This accomplished as a sort of belated Christmas present for the marque M.G., the engine was removed and overhauled. A large supercharger and external S.U. carburetor were fitted in front of the radiator in order to put the EX120 on an equal footing with a blown Austin Seven Special then being groomed in Daytona by Sir Malcolm Campbell who was also after the world speed record with his Blue Bird. Campbell had just taken (early January, 1931) the Flying Mile for Class H at 94 mph in the Austin and Eyston was out to crack 100 mph with the M.G. EX120. The best he could do was to break some lesser records.

All sorts of changes were then tried, among them various blowers and gear ratios. Finally the external S.U. carburetor was enclosed in a hasty metal covering because the bitterly cold weather was freezing the carburetor despite the alcohol in the fuel. Eyston at last took the re-tuned, modified EX120 out on the Montlhery track and put his foot down. With the tachometer reaching 7,000 rpm, records were smashed and entered in the F.I.A. books by officials who came out from Paris: Five Kilometres at 103.13 mph, Five Miles at 102.76, Ten Kilo's at 102.43 and Ten Miles at 101.87 mph. The EX120, bundled off to England, waited for a crack at the Flying Mile to be tackled later in better weather.

At Brooklands in March, 1931, Eyston won the Flying Mile but at only 97 mph. A day or so later, with the Flying Mile at 100 mph in mind and all going well, Eyston was on his way when a connecting rod let loose and destroyed the engine.

Later at the Montlhery track, the EX120 with Eyston up was to try for 100 miles in one hour. Eyston was doing nicely, averaging approximately 101 mph and taking this record handily, when he failed to see the signal telling him his one hour was over. Running another lap full bore, Eyston disappeared around the curve. When he failed to re-appear, his crew members who had noticed an ominous change in the sound of the engine set out to find him. When they reached the flaming mass that had been the EX120, Eyston was nowhere to be seen. It turned out that he had managed to extricate his considerable self from the tight cockpit and, only superficially bruised, had been picked up by a passing test driver and taken to a hospital. Eyston had another record in his pocket—but the EX-

120, a record breaker, was a charred ruin. A bearing had burned out causing a fire in the oil sump, thus ending the brief career of an exciting race car.

Though the late EX120 had been engined with the 847 cc. block in its originally intended role as prototype for the D-type Midget (Chapter 3), the record runs were all made with the 54 x 81 mm. engine. With some changing of bore and stroke dimensions, the EX120 also fulfilled prototype chores for the fabulous Type C "Montlhery" Midget which looked much like the record-breaking EX120 and, in fact, derived its nickname from the site of its forerunner's triumphs and final disaster.

When the time came again for the Double Twelve Hour Race at Brooklands in May, 1931, the starting grid was liberally sprinkled with M.G.s, thirteen in all—four teams and one driver mounted alone. The racing fraternity had been astonished by the performance of the Midget M-type the year before and was in for another lesson this year, particularly because the C-type's engine was in the tiny 750 cc. class. When the two twelve-hour racing days were over, the Austin teams had been thrashed as had been all of the bigger, more powerful cars such as the "sporting lorries," as Midget enthusiasts were inclined to call the big jobs.

The new C-types garnered the Team award, the *first five* places overall, and every International Class prize. The people at Abingdon-on-Thames had produced a winner.

The principal dimensions of the C-type are listed

With its windscreen folded flat and high-riding Brooklands exhaust sounding off, the M.G. Type C Montlhery racing Midget was the machine that stimulated the sporting fraternity in 1931. (M.G. Car Co. Ltd)

in the accompanying specifications, but there was, and is, much about this car that a "spec" table does not show. The frame was underslung in the rear, incorporating features of the EX120. Four-wheel brakes using 8-inch drums with all cable controls protected by armored casings were used, as was a fly-off handbrake. A small wheel adjustment within the driver's reach facilitated adjustment of the brake pedal and the handbrake. The front shock absorbers were mounted outside the body paneling for easy access during pit stops. The rear snubbers were adjustable by a knob beneath the dashboard. As on the EX120, the rear springs had no shackles and the front axle rode above the front springs. All four springs were semi-elliptic.

The engine displaced 746 cc., the block being basically like that of the preceding M-type with the 57 mm. bore retained. The overhead camshaft actuated the valves through adjustable rockers. A new crankshaft reduced the stroke to 73 mm. Inlet and exhaust ports were on the same side, the cylinder head being the A-A type common to the Type M. Compression ratio, 9.0 to 1, was unusually high in 1931. The output was 44 bhp at 6,400 rpm. With the 4-speed, non-synchromesh, close-ratio transmission running through a two-plate clutch and with a rear axle ratio of 5.375 to 1, the advertised mph per 1,000 rpm was 14.7, assuring high performance. The oil sump held 9 gallons of oil—a lesson also learned from the EX120—and a 7½-gallon reserve tank automatically supplied oil by means of a float feed. This little detail made for happy bearings, a most important consideration since the crankshaft had only two bearings and turned at extremely high speed.

For the Double Twelve Hour Race the C-types were slated to race, according to *The Autocar* of May 22, 1931, at 5,500 rpm maximum, or at about 81 mph. It is likely, however, that several exceeded this rpm figure because some consistently lapped the course at 70 mph and more and gear shifting had to be done with consequent higher engine speeds.

The fuel system was well designed, around 300 miles being the distance between fuel stops. The tank held 15 gallons and was back where it belonged beneath the boattailed rear deck. A single down-draft S.U. carburetor was used and the fuel was pumped by an arrangement of two Autopulse pumps. One pump operated normally until all but 2 gallons of fuel were used. Then the second pump was actuated by a switch on the dash to feed in the reserve.

Two coils were used in the 6-volt Lucas or Rotax ignition, one functioning as a spare with a change-switch on the dashboard, which carried a full complement of instruments. The large 8,000-rpm tachometer had the appropriate area blanked in cautioning red. On the steering column below the wheel was the ignition retard-and-advance control, a feature many wish were on ordinary cars today.

The body was of alloy, streamlined and lightweight, and bolted to the frame cross members at three places on each side. The windscreen folded flat forward of the double cowl (or "scuttle"). Deep indentations in each door and separate bucket seats made for comfort and efficiency, and were properly sporting. The occupant of the left seat had to watch out for his outboard arm because of the close proximity of the exhaust pipe which terminated above the left-rear cycle-fender in the flaring Brooklands manner.

A road exhaust system has replaced the Brooklands pipe on this beautifully restored Type C Montlhery Midget owned by the Henry Ford Museum in Greenfield Village, Dearborn, Michigan. (Joseph H. Wherry)

At 295 pounds delivered (less than $1,500 U.S.A. at the time) and ready for flat out racing, the Type C was bound to be a success. If a hair over 80 mph wasn't pleasing enough, a C Montlhery could be bought complete with a supercharger which, at 12 psi, boosted the rated output to 52.5 bhp at 6,500 rpm and the price by another 180 pounds. With blower, a different cylinder head dropped the compression ratio to 5.8 to 1.

From May, 1931, to June, 1932, the C-types were produced on order, 44 of them being built. Today a "C" is worth a fortune. Most of them shed the Montlhery radiator shroud in favor of the classic, vertical M.G. shell. As potent as they were beautiful, the C-types won the 1931 Irish Grand Prix in Dublin, the Royal Automobile Club's International Tourist Trophy at Belfast, and a host of other victories too numerous to list. These triumphs secured for the little speedster an honored place in automotive history.

The policy at the time was to develop Specials and outright racing models only *if* they could be made to pay their own way through sales to the public and incorporation of features into the bread-and-butter sports Midgets and other M.G. types. It was not until very late in 1932 that two prototypes of the next racer, the K3 Magnette, came forth. Strictly speaking, the K3, taking the engine as a base, was a racing development of the 6-cylinder Type K sports two-seaters, tourers, and saloons that entered production in October, 1932. These are covered elsewhere. The

Only forty-four Type C Montlhery Midgets were built—an outstanding over-the-counter full race machine. (Henry Ford Museum)

reasoning is supposed to have been that M.G., having swept the events in the 750 cc. class, should have a go at awards in the 1,100 cc. Class G. It was a course of action that paid off for about a year.

From March, 1933, to September, 1934, M.G. produced 33 of these fabulous models including the prototypes. Sharing basic chassis dimensions with all the 6-cylinder, Type K, two-seater sports cars, and having 13-inch, cable-operated brakes and the excellent 4-speed pre-selector transmission with the K2 variant, the K3 Magnette was the first all-out attempt to produce a racing car other than Midgets since the ill-fated Six 18/100 Mark III Tigress.

The chassis, longitudinal steel channels with tubular cross members, was generally an enlargement of the practice followed in the growing Midget tribe. To eliminate steering problems, in particular a tendency of the Midgets to wander directionally, a secondary steering arm was used with dual, short-track rods attached to each front wheel.

The K3 engine, like others in the K-type series, was essentially the well proven, 57 mm.-bore Midget block extended to make a 6-cylinder power plant. The new crankshaft had larger bearings, of course. The stroke was reduced to 71 mm. producing a displacement of 1,087 cc. Other features were an overhead camshaft, adjustable rockers, and magneto ignition. The distributor shaft and oil pump drive also ran a water pump. The production cars for 1933 had a Powerplus 9 supercharger and the 1934 models, a Marshall blower

The supercharged Type K3 Magnette, a 6-cylinder racer, could reach speeds in excess of 120 miles per hour. This is the 1934 model. (M.G. Car Co. Ltd.)

of the Rootes type. Both were mounted out in front of the radiator and driven at three-quarters of the engine speed by a reduction gear. Running the blower through the 6.2 to 1 head produced 120 bhp at 6,500 rpm, a lot of power in 1933 for a car weighing barely one ton.

The Type K3 was the first production competition car to offer a pre-selector transmission as standard equipment. The four gearbox ratios were selected by a quadrant-mounted lever on top of the gearbox. The next desired ratio could thus be selected prior to the change which was automatically made by a jab at the clutch pedal. The prototype and the 1933 models had a square rear, a 20½-gallon slab tank with a filler on each side for rapid servicing, and a spare wheel. The 1934 models had a streamlined tail with an internal shaped tank holding 24½ gallons. Both models had lightweight, aluminum-paneled bodies.

The first big competition for the K3 was the 1933 Mille Miglia in which a three-car works team was entered with such famous racing drivers as George Eyston and Count Johnny Lurani on the grid along with Lord Howe, Hugh Hamilton, Bernard Rubin, and Sir Henry Birkin. During this event the new K3s roared along at more than 110 mph beating Maseratis and others to win the team prize. K3s took second, third, and fourth places in the Junior Car Club International Trophy Race. The Italian ace, Nuvolari, drove a K3 to victory in the Ulster Tourist Trials. In the British Empire Trophy Race at Brooklands, a K3 won third place at an average speed of

106.9 mph, and another K3 with a special single-seater body and driven by R. T. Horton broke the Brooklands outer circuit Class G lap record with 115.5 mph. The next year, Horton took the Class G One Hour record at Brooklands at 117 mph.

K3 entries also won at the Mannin Beg race on the Isle of Man, the Circuit of Modena, the Swiss Grand Prix, and many lesser events. In the 1935 Le Mans race a K3 placed first in the 2-liter class, winning ninth overall. In later years, Horton's *mono-posto* K3 fell under the spell of Lt. Col. Goldie Gardner who used it to break the Class G Flying Mile at 148 mph. The K3's engine, smooth and powerful, was later used in the EX135 whose story appears in a later chapter. Racing rumor has it that the K3 would have been produced over a longer time had not the officials governing the 1934 Tourist Trials ruled out superchargers. The K3 was out as the mount of works teams. Production ceased in September, 1934.

By the end of 1933, the Type C Montlhery Midget and the newer J4 had triumphed over all comers. This pleasant circumstance could not last for long, however, due to the inherent limitations of the 2-bearing crankshaft. If M.G. success in competition was to continue in the 750 cc. class, a huskier engine was essential. This was borrowed from the new Type P Midget sports cars. The result was the brief production series of eight Type Q racers built between May and October, 1934. A price of 550 pounds ready to race was enticing but there were few buyers.

The Type Q racing Midget engine was a version of

the new, tougher, 3-bearing crankshaft, overhead-cam-shaft engine designed by H. N. Charles for the PA-type Midget sports cars just going into production. The stroke of the PA engine was reduced from 83 to 73 mm. to keep the displacement at 746 cc. With a Zoller Q4 supercharger out front driven through re-duction gears at 69 per cent of engine speed and pro-viding a boost of 25-28 pounds psi through one 1⅞ inch S.U. carburetor, the output was 113 bhp at 7,200 rpm. An automatic slipping device in the form of a clutch working on the flywheel to eliminate racing stress enabled the quick gear-changing capabilities of the pre-selector gearbox to be retained without dam-age to the power train. Due to the available power, it was decided to add a bit more wheelbase for better high-speed handling. Consequently, the Q Midget emerged on a 94³⁄₁₆-inch wheelbase (like the K3). Brakes were 12-inch drums. The tread, though, was 3 inches less at 45 inches.

The narrow, aluminum-sheathed body lacked doors, as did the K3, and of the eight produced, none had lights or fenders. Type Q looked very much like its 6-cylinder, 1,087 cc. predecessor. The boattail concealed 19 gallons of fuel including 4 in reserve. Weighing a scant 1,500 pounds, the Q-type set the class track record with 122.4 mph at Brooklands and consistently lapped in excess of 110 mph. The Q raised the class standing mile to more than 85 mph and late in 1934 averaged 76.3 mph at Montlhery for twenty-four hours.

So powerful was the Q Midget racer that few drivers

Another special racing Midget was the Type Q, a supercharged 746 cc. hurricane. (British Motor Corp.)

are said to have dared to capitalize on its potential. The rigid axles and semi-elliptic springs all around, though well snubbed, caused wheelspin due to the high torque and some handling problems at high speeds. Thus, in October of 1934, after barely six months of production, the Type Q was discontinued when Cecil Kimber realized that the traditional M.G. chassis designs needed improvement for big-time racing.

Kimber and staff decided that the four-wheel independent suspension systems coming into racing vogue on the continent offered the answer to high speed safety. H. N. Charles was again handed the assignment. The Midget Type R evolved, a revolutionary car in every respect excepting engine and drive train.

The engine was the now proven 746 cc. unit as used in the Type Q with compression ratio slightly decreased from 6.4 to 6.2 to 1 and a change from the coil to a Lucas magneto ignition system. The Wilson pre-selector, 4-speed transmission was retained with the overload automatic slip device, but the gear change quadrant and short lever were relocated to the steering column. With a Zoller 4RA blower running at a 28 psi boost, the bhp was 110 at 6,500 rpm; and with the standard 4.125 to 1 rear axle gears, 20.2 mph was listed per 1,000 rpm.

The power layout was in familiar M.G. territory but the frame and suspension was new ground, and on this score it is a pity that the Type R was never to

Most revolutionary M.G. of all time was the Type R Midget shown at speed on the Accerbo course in Pescara, Italy, in 1935 with Reggie Tongue up. Note the outward lean of the wheels, a characteristic of the Type R. (British Motor Corp.)

see complete development. The frame was beautiful, and is so today more than thirty years later.

Weighing only about fifty-seven pounds, the frame was a single unit fabricated of 16-gauge steel plates welded into box sections and finally integrated into a Y-shape. One channel steel cross member at the front and tubular internal bracing added stiffness. Lightening holes throughout this structure did not adversely affect the rigidity. The engine, two-plate clutch with automatic slipping device, and Wilson transmission were mounted between the forward frame

The bare bones of the Type R special racing Midget show the four-wheel independent suspension by torsion bars. (*The Motor*)

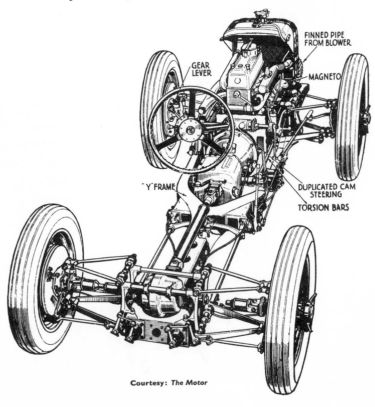

Courtesy: *The Motor*

arms. The open propeller shaft extended aft slightly above the wide stem of the frame. Final drive gears were straight cut in the usual M.G. practice and the differential cage was securely bolted to the top of the extreme rear of the frame.

The familiar rigid axles of previous M.G. types gave way to dual wishbone brackets for each wheel, front and rear. A longitudinal torsion bar, splined on each end, was secured on each side to the lower front wishbone near the latter's hinge point immediately inboard of the frame. Similarly, each rear torsion bar was rigidly attached to each bottom rear wishbone. The torsion bars were then secured to the frame in brackets permitting adjustment of the tension. Lightweight, adjustable Luvax hydraulic shock absorbers plus built-in stops to prevent undue wishbone movements completed the radical suspension.

The steering gear was actually a dual system, each front wheel having its own drop arm operating out of the centered steering gear box that was secured to a bulkhead at the immediate rear of the engine block. The front wheels were *not* connected by a tie rod. In the rear, the drive from the crown wheel of the differential to each wheel was by a short shaft with a universal joint on each end. Thus, the vertical movement of either rear wheels or front due to the road surface determined the amount of movement of the associated torsion bar. Four-wheel, cable-operated, 12-inch-diameter brakes filled most of the open space behind 18-inch, knock-off wire wheels. The wheelbase was 90½ inches, the front tread, 46⅜, and the rear tread, 45½ inches.

The body of light alloy was narrow and contained but one seat. In front, the familiar M.G. radiator shell slanted steeply and external fillers for water and the one-gallon reserve oil tank were atop the hood to quicken pit-stop times. There was no windscreen but the cowl swept sharply upward. The streamlined tail concealed the 21-gallon fuel tank which had a reserve of ¾ gallon.

The Type R was introduced early in April, 1935, and immediately won its class the first time out in the International Trophy Race at Brooklands. This was followed by winning the 1,100 cc. class in the French Grand Prix, a fifth place plus four other awards in the British Empire Trophy Race, and other awards at Berne, Switzerland, and Coppa Acerbo, Pescara, Italy.

By the end of June, ten Type R racers had been built. The independent suspension seemed to have been the solution to keeping the rear wheels on the ground during the rapid acceleration of the diminutive 1,400 pound Midget, and at high speeds which sometimes exceeded 120 mph. Enthusiasts were looking forward to seeing M.G. works teams win races during the season.

Then the bomb dropped! Sir William Morris, under whom the M.G. Car Company Ltd. had thrived as a privately owned firm, sold M.G. to Morris Motors Ltd. which was publicly owned and of which Morris was chairman of the board. Sir William and his board decreed that *all* M.G. works-sponsored racing cease immediately.

Cecil Kimber, as can be imagined, was crushed but he stayed on only to resign early in World War II. He died in a train wreck in February, 1945. Chief designer H. N. Charles, however, resigned at once. It is likely that the revolutionary single-seater Type R racing Midget which had departed so radically from the traditional sports car field had much to do with the decision to stop racing. Thus, the Type R survived in only the ten cars built. These raced in private hands for a few years, then drifted into collections. The type was the most promising of all the Kimber-inspired all-out racers. Many have mourned its passing in the three intervening decades, for there is no telling to what heights the M.G. works banner might have been carried.

SPECIFICATIONS

Type and Name	Cylinders	Bore and Stroke (mm.)	Displacement (cc.)	Compression Ratio ($1/m$ to 1)	Supercharged	Brake Horsepower @ rpm	Transmission Speeds	Gear Ratios and Alternates (if any)	Rear Axle Ratios and Alternates (if any)	Tires	Wheelbase (inches)	Tread, Front and Rear
C Monthlery Midget	4	57 x 73	746	5.8 5.0	yes no	52.5 @ 6,500 44 @ 6,400	4	1.00 1.36 1.86 2.69	5.375 5.50	19 x 4.00	81	42
K3 Magnette	6	57 x 71	1,087	6.2	yes	120 @ 6,500	4 Pre*	1.00 1.36 2.32 4.18	5.78 4.89 4.33	19 x 4.75	94 3/16	48
Q Midget	4	57 x 73	746	6.4	yes	113 @ 7,200	4 Pre	1.00 1.00 1.36 1.31 2.00 1.84 3.40 3.097	4.50 4.875 4.125	18 x 4.75	94 3/16	45
R Midget	4	57 x 73	746	6.2	yes	110 @ 6,500	4 Pre	1.00 1.31 1.84 3.097	4.125 4.50 4.875	18 x 4.75	90 1/2	46 3/8 45 1/2

* "Pre" indicates *Pre-selector* transmission.

3 The Mighty Midgets

WHEN a new 847 cc. engine was developed by Morris Motors, it was inevitable that Cecil Kimber and his associates at the M.G. works would obtain one for experiments. A production engine such as this with an already well-developed overhead camshaft offered extensive applications in small sports cars. Furthermore, the diminutive Morris Minor, powered by this engine, was selling well. So why shouldn't an M.G. sports car be based upon the small Morris? This was how the M.G. was launched as a marque.

Precisely what all the alterations were, the special tuning and the like, that improved the Minor's engine is obscure. It is enough to say that when the new model was introduced in April, 1929, it was an immediate hit. Obviously, the only right name for the

The 1929 Morris Minor was the basis for the first M.G. Midget. (British Motor Corp.)

midget was "Midget." For other reasons, also obscure, it was christened Type M. The letter and name went together, so it went into the works record books as the Type M Midget. No one at the time could have foreseen that the tiny machine, with a cloth-covered plywood body on a 78-inch wheelbase, was to be the first of a long line of the world's most popular sports cars. Not underslung as some later Midget types would be, the springs were shackle mounted all around.

Several of the sporting group close to Kimber were excited by what they saw. The frame of steel channels had leaf springs at all corners. Whether anyone outside the works knew that the universal joints had *fabric* discs is not recorded. The fuel tank, almost in the driver's lap beneath the bonnet, was certainly not the sort of arrangement one would yearn for in a competition car, nor would one specify a 2-bearing crankshaft. But with the weight pared to a minimum, about 1,100 pounds at the ready, with lightweight, 19-inch wire wheels and big, friction shock absorbers holding down the unsprung weight, the new Midget M proved a fast and roadable mount.

The compression ratio of 4.5 to 1 was sufficiently docile to allow further development, and the 20 bhp at 4,000 rpm couldn't fail to provide good performance. So, with the 1929 High Speed Trials, a feature of the Junior Car Club's annual Members Day at Brooklands, scheduled for the next month, it was decided to enter a team of three Midgets. M.G. was going for broke. One of the cars was driven by the Earl of March and

The first of all M.G. Midgets was the diminutive Type M. (British Motor Corp.)

he had a reputation for having good teammates. The works supplied their top mechanics to ride along since the custom of the time called for two aboard.

Even with preparation and practice time at a minimum, the three new M-type Midgets scattered the opposition and won the team award. M-type sales climbed.

Then various enthusiasts approached the works with the next year's Double Twelve Hour Race in mind. Kimber was agreeable—the Austin Sevens had had things their way long enough. H. N. Charles took on the assignment, along with development of the 18/100 Mark III Tigress, of masterminding changes to increase the output. The compression ratio was increased a bit, the crankshaft and connecting rods were strengthened and balanced, inlet and exhaust ports polished, tougher valve springs installed and additional support was given to the rocker arm shaft. All this raised the outside maximum safety limits to well over 5,000 rpm. Valve timing was improved also by allowing about 7 degrees of overlap at top dead center. Bench tests revealed a gain in output which was now 27 bhp at a safe 4,500 rpm.

On May 9 and 10, 1930, the re-worked M-type Midgets—the works team and two independent entries, one piloted by a lady—upset the Austins which were running with superchargers. Average speeds for the twenty-four hours of racing, twelve each day, ranged from 57.7 to 60.23 mph. Most remarkable, the transmission had but three speeds, but the Midgets won their class team award and placed variously from fourteenth to twentieth overall.

Later in the season, the private entry of F. H. B. Samuelson and F. R. Kindell in their Midget M in the Belgian Twenty-Four Hour Race at Spa, the lone British entry in any class, took fifth place in the 1,100 cc. class. The Midget Ms had deeply cut-out doors and almost always raced with cycle mudguards, and windshield folded flat.

After the victory in the Double Twelve Hour Race— the waterloo of the 18/100 Mark III Tigress as already seen—the modifications so successfully proven became a part of the standard specifications of the Type M Midget. As a result of this race, the figures 12/12 became part of the little speedster's name. (In 1931 the C-type Montlhery would raise the M.G. banner higher.)

Late in 1930, light metal panels replaced the fabric over wood on the bodies, and a "Sportsmen's Coupe," also a two-seater with cycle fenders but with sliding windows and a luggage boot, was marketed. By July, 1932, about 3,200 M-type Midgets had been made. As was usual at the M.G. works, even better things were in store and by the time the *first* of the Midget type came to the end of the production line, other types were already crowding each other.

Described sometimes as a four-seater tourer development of the Type M and also as a sports version of the Type C Montlhery racing M.G., the Type D Midget was, in fact, a distinctive and considerably different vehicle, although owing much to its two famous forerunners. When brought out in October, 1931,

To the surprise of many, the fabric-bodied Type M Midget proved a first class competition sports car on track or highway. (British Motor Corp.)

A four-seater development of the Type M was the Type D Midget, a family sports car on an 84-inch chassis. (British Motor Corp.)

in time for the London Show and in response to a need for a family sportster, the wheelbase was 84 inches and the gearbox had three speeds with ratios identical to those in the M-type. After the first hundred cars, a 4-speed transmission was made available as an extra cost option and the wheelbase was increased to 86 inches.

The styling was definitely sporting with the channel steel frame slung beneath the rigid axles on fairly flat leaf springs which were pivoted on shackles at the front and trunnion-mounted at the rear ends. Knock-off rather than bolted-on 19-inch wire wheels, heavier pointed fenders, exterior handles on the two notched doors, front bucket seats and a rear bench suitable for children made a very dashing and practical vehicle. The metal sheathing on the hardwood-framed body was moderately rounded in the rear where the spare wheel was racked. In appearance, the D-type Midget was not unlike the Type F Magna.

The engine was much like the original unit in the EX120 which displaced 847 cc. Rugged but with few refinements—inlet and exhaust valve ports were on a common side, for example—the output was the same as that of the Type M engine: 27 bhp at 4,500 rpm. The engine used a single S.U. carburetor and coil ignition, and had a compression ratio of 5.4 to 1. Tests revealed that, due to weight, performance at the low end was limited.

Roadability, however, was excellent with rack and pinion steering, a man-sized 16½-inch wheel and a low center of gravity despite a relatively heavy body. Ready-for-the-road weight was about 1,480 pounds for the open tourer; with an optional saloon body, the weight was in the neighborhood of 1,600 pounds. For its power, the D-type Midget was a bit heavy. The M.G. works quoted 14.7 mph per 1,000 rpm so one could count, with patience, on 65–66 mph at best, on the slow side for an M.G. The fuel tank, beneath the sheet metal, carried 4 gallons plus 2 in reserve and the wet oil sump held 4 quarts.

In production only seven months, 250 units of the Type D had been built when production ceased making this sports tourer one of the rarer of the Midgets. With more power, the Type D could conceivably have brought motoring sports to more single-car families. That day was not far away.

When the Type J began coming off the assembly line in July, 1932, it started the blood stirring in sports car fans and, to the present day, this Midget model has enjoyed a following far out of proportion to the 5,530 built. Production ended in January, 1934. The Type J had the advantage of a reasonable weight of 1,260 pounds moved along by the improved, opposed inlet and exhaust port, 847 cc. engine. Knowledgeable drivers treated the 2-bearing crankshaft engine with respect lest the crank be tempted to twist out of line. Keeping an eye on oil pressure was essential, for the sump carried only 4 quarts (until the advent of the special racing J4 version which had a float-fed 2-quart reserve). Maintaining the engine with care assured

The Type J2 Midget is a favorite everywhere. Owner-restorer of this example, Mr. Jarl de Boer, is behind the wheel of his treasure in Walnut Creek, California. This is a later J2 with metal-sheathed body. (Joseph H. Wherry)

There is plenty of working space beneath the bonnet of Mr. de Boer's J2 Midget as seen from the right side where dual S.U. carburetors feed a potent 847 cc. engine. Note the accelerator pedal behind the firewall where all driving controls are within easy reach for servicing. (Joseph H. Wherry)

keen owners a genuine 75 mph in the two-seater J2 when they allowed their mount the bridle, but not for too long. Speeds in first through third gears were approximately 19, 38, and 62 mph. Top gear was extremely flexible, permitting under 10 mph with the

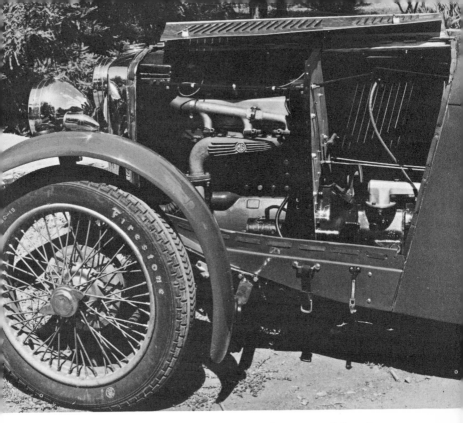

The exhaust manifold, marked with the M.G. octagon, below the water circulating pipe alongside the overhead camshaft cover fills the left side of the engine compartment on the Type J2 Midget. (Joseph H. Wherry)

ignition retarded. Dual 1-inch S.U. carburetors were fitted and the compression ratio was an improved 6.2 to 1 in the most numerous J1 four-seater tourers and salonettes and J2 two-seater models. Transmissions were 4-speed synchromesh and ignition was by coil.

Thus improved, the output was 36 bhp at 5,500 rpm. *The Autocar* credited this engine with a safe 5,800 rpm range, however. The driver sat low with legs nearly straight forward, and feet almost touching the fuel pump.

The body, though wood framed (as were all M.G. sports cars until comparatively recently), was kept as light as possible with deeply notched doors and non-adjustable seats with a one-piece backrest in the J2. The dashboard was double-cowled and had two large instrument groupings, octagonal in outline, with the combined speedometer and tachometer directly in front of the driver. All J-types had flat folding wind-screens and, naturally, cycle fenders.

The chassis consisted of the classic channel steel and tubular crosspieces with the traditional leaf springs, shackle-mounted at the front ends and secured by bronze trunnions at the rear ends, snubbed tightly with friction shocks. Large 19-inch wire wheels, center-locked on an 86-inch wheelbase, were standard as were 8-inch-diameter brake drums on all J1, J2, and J3 models. Brakes on the rare J4 were 12-inch drums while all models had a racing type fly-off handbrake. Close-coupled, the length overall was just 124 inches.

The J3 and J4 models had engines destroked to 746 cc. Only thirty were built, supercharged versions of the J2 roadster. The J3 had a 5.2 to 1 compression ratio and a 6A Powerplus supercharger mounted simi-larly to the blower on the K3 Magnette. The works has never specified the output. Excellent trials cars, a J3 was awarded the coveted Coupe des Glaciers in the Alpine International in 1933 and won several International Class H records at Montlhery.

The better known J4 had a compression ratio of 5.5 to 1, a fully counterbalanced special crankshaft, and with a more powerful blower, delivered a husky 72.3 bhp at 6,000 rpm. Introduced in March, 1933, the J4 was overshadowed by the Type K3 Magnette 6-cyl-

Tachometer and speedometer are combined in the large dial directly in front of the driver on the strictly functional dashboard of the J2 Midget. The thick rim of the spring steel wheel eliminates that clenched-fist feeling. (Joseph H. Wherry)

inder racer which bowed almost simultaneously. The first of the J4 victories was a class win in the hill climb event at the German Grand Prix in 1933 with the famed Hugh Hamilton at the wheel. A J4 came in third in the Isle of Man Mannin Beg Race the same year and garnered first place in a 100-mile race at Southport. In the 1933 Ulster Tourist Trials, a Royal Automobile Club event of importance, Hamilton's J4 finished less than a minute behind the more powerful K3 Magnette with an average of a fraction over 73 mph for the entire race.

As was the case with many sports cars of the thirties —other marques as well as the subject car—styling variations occurred within a single type. Some of the J1 tourers and salonettes had swept fenders, but most had lines much like those of the Type D Midget and the Type F 6-cylinder Magna. Some of the J2 types had external door handles while others did not, and there were minor differences in the external wedge-shaped fuel tanks. Fuel capacity was 9 plus 3 reserve gallons on all models except the full race J4 which carried 4 plus 2 in reserve. On the J2, fuel consumption, even with fairly hard driving, generally produced upward of thirty miles per gallon. The sports models had well muffled road exhausts with tailpipes beneath the chassis; but the competition J3 and J4 types had the regulation Brooklands exhaust which was capable of deafening the ears within a wide radius. Records fell to this Midget, too. Late in February, 1932, a works-prepared J3 running a big blower and with

Variations in minor details were common on early Midgets; note that this J2 owned by Mr. de Boer has no exterior door latch handles and that the ends of the fuel tank are fluted. (Joseph H. Wherry)

This J2 Midget has exterior door latches and smooth ends on the gas tank. (M.G. Car Co. Ltd.)

George Eyston at the wheel shattered all of the International Class H records which the EX127 (Chapter 6) had not already taken to give M.G. a clean sweep.

Probably the most sensational performance of the J4 was placing sixth overall at Le Mans in 1934, while the high point might have been the 1934 Tourist Trophy Race. But, like the K3 Magnette, the J4 was ruled out by the ban on superchargers.

For a price of 200 pounds for a J2 roadster, a whisker under $1,000 U.S.A. money at the time, one could scarcely go wrong. The open and closed four-seater J1 models were slightly higher, and the blown J3 and J4 competition types, of course, nearly twice as costly. As to speed, the J4 is said to have been capable of close to 120 mph. For 1933, such performance with 750 cc. thrashing a 2-bearing crankshaft was terrific— and would be good even today.

Though marvelously roadworthy, the popular Types J1 and J2 were raucous to the ear and rough to ride in. They were fun to drive, yet improvements were needed. Abingdon simultaneously phased out the Type J and began producing the new Type P in January, 1934. Outsiders would not have been impressed by the P-type Midget. It looked like a small edition of the Type L Magna even to the rear fenders which terminated above the level of the rear axle with the machine at rest and unladen. The new car was the *first* Midget to have a running board.

Of the two Type P models, the PA was produced from January, 1934, to July, 1935. The latter date,

Possibly the most beautifully styled in the classic tradition of all the Midgets were the Type P models; this is the PB. (British Motor Corp.)

From the side, the sweeping lines of the the PA Midget with "Airline Coupe" coachwork by Carbodies of Coventry are evident. Mr. Gert Orla Jensen of Berkeley, California, is the owner. (G. O. Jensen)

as mentioned previously, is of immense importance in M.G. sports car history: the takeover of M.G. by Morris Motors, the immediate ban on factory-sponsored racing, and the end of Type PA production all happened at once. It was two months before another Midget was in production, the PB assembly line being active from September, 1935, until May, 1936. Close to 2,500 Types PA and PB were built as two-seater roadsters, four-seater tourers, and the Airline Coupe with coachwork by Carbodies of Coventry. The latter was smart, comfortable, and rakish with the spare wheel recessed in the rear deck. Only 100 Airlines were built.

Loud were the cries of anguish when the P-type replaced the beloved Type J, particularly the J2. The

The spare wheel of the Type PA Midget "Airline Coupe" is recessed in the steeply sloped rear deck. (G. O. Jensen)

P-types were truly "born to trouble," but they proved out well. They raced occasionally but proved their mettle in the rough trials and bashes that preceded the war. Now, more than thirty years later, either of the P-types is eagerly sought. The PA two-seater was 7 inches longer overall at 131 inches than the J2, had a slightly longer wheelbase at $87\frac{5}{16}$ inches, and was about 225 pounds heavier at 1,652 pounds. The tread was not changed. Though the frame design followed prior practice, all members were heavier and the PA, again compared with the J2, was considerably sturdier in every respect. Just what had the Kimber group done with the PA to merit criticism by those who thought the J2 without possible equal? Frankly, nothing but good.

Beginning with the engine, the two 1-inch diameter S.U. carburetors and the bore and stroke dimensions were unchanged. The compression ratio at 6.2 to 1, was one full point higher, and down out of sight was a completely new and much stronger 3-bearing crankshaft, the *first* ever in a Midget. The oil sump held 5 gallons without apparent need of a reserve and there was an external oil filter. The cooling system held 11½ quarts, 1½ more than the J2, and, like the latter, had no water pump. With the same displacement but so many improvements, one would think that the

The "Airline Coupe" body was also available on the 6-cylinder NA Magnette. (G. O. Jensen)

output would have been increased. But the PA engine developed the same 36 bhp at 5,500 rpm as the J2.

Why not more? Several factors were responsible for this seeming design fallibility: the crankshaft was heavier, stronger, and had one more bearing; the block was also a bit heavier for that reason and the entire valve gear was beefed up. But, what the engine of the PA did not gain in output, it more than gained in durability. The power curve had to be superior to that of the J2 engine for, despite the extra 225 pounds of total weight, the maximum speed of the PA was virtually the same as that of the J2—from about 72 to 75 or so mph. Furthermore, the PA was a superior handling car and was quieter, and safer because of the 12-inch brakes on all models.

After the M.G. Car Company underwent the big shakeup in July, 1935, the improved Type PB Midget began to take shape. When it was introduced, the improvements incorporated were as mechanically extensive, and just as invisible on the surface, as those of the PA had been.

Using the same design engine block, the bore was increased 3 mm. for a displacement of 939 cc. and the cylinder head was shaved to increase the compression ratio to 6.8 to 1. The ignition timing was unchanged at 20 degrees before top dead center but the valve timing was identical to that of the PA. The output of the larger engine, however, was up 6 horsepower to 43 bhp at the same 5,500 rpm. Frame, overall weight, suspension, and other factors were unchanged; consequently the PB turned out to be an 80 mph maximum vehicle, with windshield folded, at no sacrifice in durability or safety tolerances.

With respect to styling, one had to look closely to discover differences between the PA and the later PB. The PB introduced the vertically slatted radiator grille to the marque, a smart finishing touch to the familiar honeycomb of the cooling core. To all practical ends, the only change of consequence in interior appearance was the instrument layout: the PA dashboard was very like that of the late J2 whereas the PB tachometer, very large and inside an octagonal rim, was located in front of the driver while the speedometer was smaller and relocated to the passenger's side in a matching instrument cluster.

The Midget was maturing and the interior was reflecting the customers' demand for more everyday, go-to-work comfort without compromising the handling qualities required of a true sports car. The PA became a desirable mount in trials and hill climbs and raced, now and then, in the hands of private owners.

The PB was an even better trials car with its closer ratio gearbox. No options were listed for transmission ratios but the same three rear axle gear choices were available for either P-type. By the time the last PB was put together in May, 1936, owners were discovering the susceptibility of either the PA or PB engine to judicious tuning. Superchargers, usually low pressure units, found their way into the position forward of the radiator and performances increased proportionately. One cycle-fendered trials team, with super-charged PB Midgets painted deliciously in cream and brown, the official M.G. colors, won award after award during 1936–1937 in the most bone-bending of all motor sports. Other supercharged PB Specials have topped 100 mph without undue strain.

It would seem that the greatest single blessing be-stowed by either the PA or PB should have been con-fidence commensurate with the obvious superiority of the 3-bearing crankshaft over the long used 2-bearing installation in all previous Midgets. This factor plus the other attributes made the P-types the best all-around Midgets of the time. Enthusiasts are legion who still contend that the PA and PB were the best looking, best all-around M.G.s of the pre-war period.

The P-types were the *last* of the single overhead cam-shaft Midgets. Three months later the advent of the first of the Type T Midgets precipitated more wailing because Abingdon had let down the bars to modern design!

In July, 1936, it happened. An M.G. Midget with box-section chassis longerons, a pushrod engine more than a third of a liter larger than any previous Midget's powerplant, an air-cleaner as standard equipment, and hydraulic brakes, of all things, was placed on sale. This upstart in the well organized sports car world—today a favored vintage sports car—was the *first* of the revolu-tionary T-types, the TA.

That there had been a break with Midget tradition in the new TA was evident in the overall length of

143 inches, a whole foot longer; and at 56 inches in width, the TA was nearly 4 inches wider. Once the skeptic was seated inside the two-seater roadster, however, he could not fail to notice that the individual seat cushions were softer and 2½ inches wider than the 15-inchers in the Type P, and that the full 38 inches of headroom allowed an extra 3 inches for a hat. From the foot pedals there were 36 inches-plus total leg room in the TA and here, so the traditionalists said, the PA had it all over the new, larger Midget with 41 inches of leg space. Touché, but was it necessary to be able to drive with both legs in long straight splints? After all, the width of the scuttle in the TA was 39½ inches, nearly 5 inches more than in the PA. And so the pros and cons all but obscured the meat of the new Midget that was to be sire to nearly fifty thousand T-types, carry the light, sports car message to the New World, and be instrumental in upsetting all the vested, pet theories about small cars and sports machines in particular.

When an open two-seater PA, now staunchly defended by the same people who had once compared it unkindly with the J2, was placed on the scale with a new TA opposite, the latter outweighed its elder brother by well over 100 pounds. The new TA open two-seater weighed 1,765 pounds and with reason: the wheelbase was 94 inches and the tread was 45. But that was only half the story; the rest lay beneath the bonnet. The new 1,292 cc. engine was the first ever in a Midget with the overhead valves actuated by

The Type TA Midget set the style for the famed post-war machines which electrified the sports car scene in America. (British Motor Corp.)

pushrods, the first to exceed 1 liter in swept volume, the first to have the generator driven by a belt rather than by a crankshaft drive, the first with a cooling system thermostat. The TA was the first Midget sports car to develop 50 bhp at 4,500 rpm.

True, the overhead camshaft was gone but so were most of the noises and tuning problems. The ignition and valve timing was mild though sufficient. The familiar 1-inch-diameter, dual S.U. carburetors were present, as was the 6.5 to 1 compression ratio, higher than in any previous Midget except in the PB being replaced.

New owners discovered that the more rigid, box-section frame members resisted stresses even better, and that the T-type's body, still wood framed, required less maintenance to prevent it from coming apart in the trials, which were gaining in popularity. Even the famed "Cream Cracker" team switched and found that the TA had what mud-bashing required.

A choice of three bodies was offered, all carrying forward the styling of the P-type: a two-seater roadster, an Airline Coupe, and a lovely drop-head coupe by Tickford. The polished walnut dashboard was under a double cowl, but something was lacking—the octagonal rims of the two instrument dials. The instruments were there—in large circles. The windscreens still folded flat, the roadster had a proper slab fuel tank holding 12 gallons plus 3 in reserve, and the knock-off wire wheels were a full 19 inches across.

A rating of 16.7 mph was quoted per 1,000 rpm, and

The Autocar for September 18, 1936, reported timed two-way runs over a quarter mile in excess of 77 mph without tinkering with the tuning. Gear speeds attained on the 4-speed box—synchromesh on third and top—were 17–23, 29–39, and 50–61 in first through third respectively.

Acceleration was improved too: from a standing start to 30 mph in 6.1 seconds and to 60 mph in 23.1 seconds. These were carefully timed true speeds. Rack and pinion steering and the suspension were in the M.G. tradition, leaf springs and rigid axles all around plus hydraulic brakes in 9-inch drums. Handling in every respect was improved, especially on wet blacktop and rutty roads. The prices were up a bit, too, the lowest being 222 pounds for the open two-seater. This was the car that Johnny Phillip Morris brought to America just before World War II.

In May, 1939, the M.G. works brought out the even peppier Type TB Midget. Principal specifications followed those of the TA but there was a new engine —the record-bred, and now famous, XPAG unit. With a higher compression ratio of 7.3 to 1 and larger 1¼-inch carburetors, displacement was less (1,250 cc.), the result of a larger 66.5 mm. bore and a shorter 90 mm. stroke. The transmission now was synchronized on all but first gear. Whereas the TA clutch was a single-plate, cork-faced unit immersed in oil, the TB had a dry clutch. Brake horsepower was 54.4 at 5,200 rpm. The lower ratio rear axle, 5.125 instead

A reference point for distinguishing between the nearly identically styled TA and TB models is the chromed stud on each end of the gas tank. This is the TB Midget. (British Motor Corp.)

of 4,875 to 1, reduced the speed per 1,000 rpm in top gear slightly to 15.8 mph.

Modified timing, even less fussy, and a new counter-balanced crankshaft allowed higher engine speeds; and the TB roadster, about 25 pounds lighter, was easily capable of reaching 80 mph and of cruising hours on end close to the mile-a-minute mark.

The TB, however, was not long for the production line where it replaced the TA. The line was closed in September, 1939, after a total 3,400 TA and TB types were built, to produce no more Midgets until after hostilities ceased nearly six years later. Then, Midgets cast in the image of Types TA and TB were produced, the subject of a later chapter.

Type and Name	Cylinders	Bore and Stroke (mm.)	Displacement (cc.)	Compression Ratio (1/1 to 1)	Supercharged	Brake Horsepower @ rpm	Transmission Speeds	Gear Ratios and Alternates (if any)	Rear Axle Ratios and Alternates (if any)	Tires	Wheelbase (inches)	Tread, Front and Rear
M Midget	4	57 x 83	847	4.5	no	20 @ 4,000	3	1.00 1.83 3.50		19 x 4.00	78	42
M 12/12 Midget	4	57 x 83	847	prob-ably 5.4	no	27 @ 4,500	3	1.00 1.83 3.50		19 x 4.00	78	42
D Midget	4	57 x 83	847	5.4	no	27 @ 4,500	3 alt. 4	1.00 1.83 3.50 (not stated for alt. 4-speed)	5.375	19 x 4.00	84 early 86 later	42
J1 Midget	4	57 x 83	847	6.2	no	36 @ 5,500	4	1.00 {1.00}	5.375	19 x 4.00	86	42
J2 Midget	4	57 x 83	847	6.2	no	36 @ 5,500	4	1.36 J4 {1.36}	5.375	19 x 4.00	86	42
J3 Midget	4	57 x 73	746	5.2	yes	not stated	4	2.14 only {1.86}	4.780	19 x 4.00	86	42
J4 Midget	4	57 x 73	746	5.5	yes	72.3 @ 6,000	4	3.58 {2.69}	5.375	19 x 4.50	86	42
PA Midget	4	57 x 83	847	6.2	no	36 @ 5,500	4	1.00 1.36 (no alt. 2.32 stated) 4.18	5.375 or 5.125	19 x 4.00	87⁵⁄₁₆	42
PB Midget	4	60 x 83	939	6.8	no	43 @ 5,500	4	1.00 1.42 2.20 3.715	5.875	19 x 4.00	87⁵⁄₁₆	42
TA Midget	4	63.5 x 102	1,292	6.5	no	50 @ 4,500	4	1.00 1.32 2.04 3.454	4.875	19 x 4.50	94	45
TB Midget	4	66.5 x 90	1,250	7.3	no	54.4 @ 5,200	4	1.00 1.35 1.95 3.38	5.125	19 x 4.50	94	45

4. More 6-Cylinder M.G.s and the Touch of Luxury

TWO factors were responsible for the production, during the 1930's, of an interesting and sometimes bewildering assortment of 6-cylinder M.G. cars: the smashing appeal of the Midgets for buyers of modest means, and a fund of engineering and production experience. By late 1931, it was obvious that the market for well appointed 6-cylinder tourers and saloons would soon be lacking M.G. representation.

Consequently, Kimber reasoned that a new Six was about due, that it should possess sporting characteristics but be a bit less costly than the 18/80 models, and that it should be introduced in the autumn of 1931 in the London Show along with the new Midget. The 4-cylinder Midgets would be the cake, the luxury Six types, the frosting.

The little 4-cylinder engine with bore and stroke of 57 and 83 mm. respectively (as in the Type M Midget) had proven itself capable of extensive modifications and, hence, there were no great obstacles to adding two cylinders. For the F-type Magna, this bore and stroke gave 1,271 cc. displacement. With overhead camshaft, dual 1-inch, horizontal S.U. carburetors and coil ignition, 37.2 bhp at 4,100 rpm was developed. The resulting Type F Magna was officially introduced in October, 1931, the first of six distinct types of quality Sixes, with numerous variants, that would keep M.G. in a wider market.

The chassis of the Type F Magna, channel steel with the familiar tubular cross members, was a virtual duplicate of its Midget counterpart, the Type D covered in Chapter 3, except that it was longer to accommodate the 6-cylinder engine. The 42-inch tread of the F permitted the use of suspension, axles, and running gear that were nearly identical to those of the Midget D. The transmission, however, had four speeds and was the same type E.N.V. box, with altered gear ratios, that had been proven on the C-type Montlhery Midget racer.

Styling was sporting in all three models, with bodies framed in hardwood and sheathed with metal, and tasteful interiors with leather upholstery and wood-paneled dashboards. The F1 was a four-seater tourer with a slanting tail end having an internal fuel tank holding 4 gallons plus 2 in reserve, and spare wheel. The doors were conventional, and the fenders carried

The Type F Magna was produced in a variety of open and closed models, with family-sized four-seaters predominating, for the "light six" market. Shown is the F2 model. (British Motor Corp.)

out the sporting theme with a modified style similar to but fuller than the spartan cycle types.

The F2 was a two-seater roadster with deeply notched doors, spare cycle fenders, and a flat tail end with an external slab tank containing nine gallons plus 3 reserve.

The F3 was a moderately refined version with either four-seater tourer or salonette bodies, the latter having a luggage boot in the tail with a large cover hinged at the bottom.

Brakes were four-wheel drum mechanicals, cable operated, of 8-inch diameter on the F1 and 12 inch on the F2 and F3. Knock-off wire wheels were 19-inch diameter. With a standard rear axle ratio of 4.78 to 1, 16.7 mph per 1,000 rpm was listed giving a theoretical maximum speed on the order of 65–67 mph for this machine which, in four-seater tourer form, weighed about 1,725 pounds. That the F-type Magna limbered up some with tuning and service, however, is indicated by a period road test by *The Autocar* which credited it with 72.5 mph. Prices for the F-type ranged from about 250 to 300 pounds.

In production about fourteen months, around 1,250 F-type Magnas had been built when phased out in December of 1932.

Probably no M.G. Type before or since the Type K Magnette possessed a more confusing set, or sets, of specifications. There were three distinct variants mounted on chassis of two wheelbases using four engines of three displacements, each with an overhead

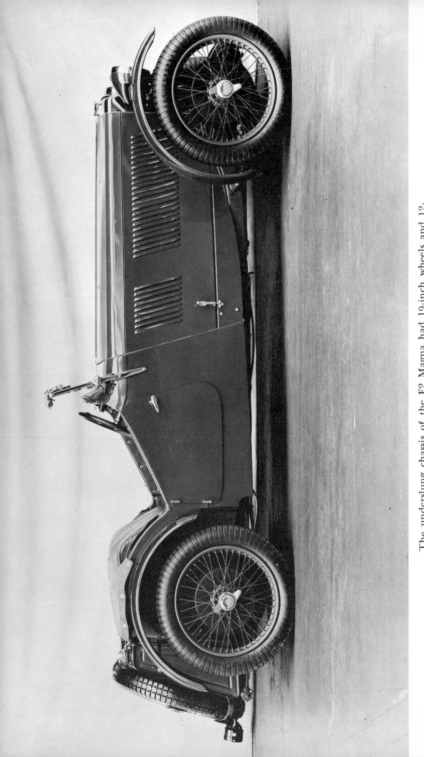

The underslung chassis of the F2 Magna had 19-inch wheels and 12-inch brakes. (British Motor Corp.)

camshaft. Types K1, K2, and KN were developments, basically, of the F-type. All employed semi-elliptical springs at each wheel and these were hung by sliding trunnions rather than by hinged shackles. Each used an open propeller shaft and the tread was 48 inches. Steering was improved by a split track rod which greatly facilitated handling. All models had 19-inch wire knock-off wheels and 13-inch diameter mechanical brakes. The transmission on each had four speeds, some being Wilson pre-selectors and others of traditional non-syncromesh type.

As for body styles, there were four and here a rule of thumb applied: all Types K1 and KN had a 108-inch wheelbase with four-seater tourer and saloon bodies, while the shorter 94¾₆-inch wheelbase chassis K2 models were two-seaters, most of them roadsters but a few being closed coupes.

The bodies were wood framed and, in this connection, the fine craftsmanship of the K1 saloons merits attention. These were *pillarless* four-door sedans. No body pillar separated front and rear doors between the sills and roof. The front doors were hinged at the front; the rear doors, at the rear. Safety for occupants of the rear seat was assured by an arrangement of latches which required that a front door be opened before the adjacent rear door could be unlatched. There were no exterior rear door latches—they opened only from inside. The saloons, incidentally, were the most popular of all K-types, many of them having

The superb coach-built body of the Type K1 Magnette four-door saloon had no central door pillar. (British Motor Corp.)

sliding roof panels. The four engines were sprinkled throughout the Type K range.

The KA engine was based upon that of the Type F Magna. The 57 mm. bore remained but the stroke was reduced to 71 mm. giving 1,087 cc. displacement. The ignition was by magneto, and three S.U. carburetors were used. Output was 39 bhp at 5,500 rpm. Valve timing was critical to prevent noise in the preselector gearbox due to vibration. This KA engine was used only in the K1 four-seaters, from introduction in October, 1932, until about the middle of 1933, giving these classic-lined cars a maximum speed of around 70 mph. This engine was the basis of the fabulous K3 racers.

The KB engine had the same bore and stroke as the KA but use of a non-synchromesh gearbox permitted better valve timing which, with the same ignition and three S.U. carburetors, slightly increased the output to 41 bhp at 5,500 rpm. This engine was used in K1 four-seaters and K2 two-seaters during the first six months of 1933.

The KD engine (there was no production KC unit) differed primarily in having an 83 mm. stroke, increasing the displacement to 1,271 cc. Retaining the magneto ignition and triple S.U. carburetors, the output was raised to a more impressive 48.5 bhp at 5,500 rpm. This engine variant was always teamed with the Wilson pre-selector transmission, but a vibration dampening auxiliary clutch between the block and the gearbox effectively eliminated the vibration that dogged the KA engine. Both short chassis K2 and long chassis K1 models used the KD powerplant from about July, 1933, to January, 1934.

About mid-1934, the fourth engine to be used in the Type K Magnette appeared. This powerplant had the specifications and output of the Type NA Magnette—discussed in its alphabetical order later in this chapter—that was being marketed simultaneously with the Type K. With this engine, the Type KN Magnette was a slightly better performer, having a maximum speed of around 75 mph. On the 108-inch wheelbase, an up-to-date version of the K1 four-seaters, the KN remained in production until very late in 1935. The epitome of good taste and consistently styled, the only concession to flamboyance was an occasional two-tone color scheme. The interior leathers were the finest, instrumentation was complete, and road manners were definitely sporting.

Despite a full three years in production, only about four hundred of all models of the Type K Magnette were built. These cars were built primarily to order for the connoisseur.

As the first Magna, the Type F, ended its production, an improved model, Type L, took its place. (Because projected designs sometimes never materialize, it is not surprising that there was no Type G, H, or I.) Introduction was in January, 1933, and some 575 cars were built during the ensuing twelve months. Production terminated in January, 1934. Open and closed two- and four-seaters comprised this series of very at-

One of the handsomest of all M.G. types, the Type K1 Magnette introduced two-color exteriors. (British Motor Corp.)

Stylewise, the Type L Magna was the 6-cylinder counterpart of the P-type Midgets in 1933–1934. (British Motor Corp.)

tractive sports cars with the open models predominating.

The new Type L Magna sat on a wheelbase of precisely the same length as the Type K2 Magnettes, a scant $\frac{3}{16}$ of an inch more than the first Magna. The 42-inch tread was the same as its Magna parent, and like that of preceding Midgets too; in fact, the axles were out of Type J Midget parts bins. The frame was in the M.G. tradition, rugged but unspectacular. The brakes, across the board, were 12-inch-diameter drums with the fly-off handbrake used on all Magnas.

The engine was the ohc 1,087 cc. unit used with such success in the K3 racer and the K1 Magnettes. Coil ignition was used with dual $1\frac{1}{8}$-inch S.U. carburetors of semi-downdraft design. The cylinder head was of opposed port design, the inlet ports on one side, the exhaust ports on the other. With 6.4 to 1 compression ratio the output was 41 bhp at 5,500 rpm—that old friend, the KB engine again—the only powerplant used in the Type L Magna. A two-plate dry clutch and a fairly close ratio, 4-speed crash transmission with a 3.58 to 1 rear axle driven by an open propeller shaft produced 15.2 mph per 1,000 rpm. Maximum speeds of 75 to 80 mph were the order with this engine, keenly tuned, in the Type L roadster which weighed approximately 1,760 pounds.

The beautiful styling paralleled that of concurrent Midgets—sweeping clamshell fenders, double-cowled dashboards with the large tachometer in front of the driver, and slab rear ends with external fuel tanks on the open roadsters and tourers. Fuel capacities were 9 gallons plus 3 reserve, and 8 and 2 reserve on the roadster and tourer respectively.

All the bodies were wood-framed with metal paneling. The prices reflected good value: two-seater roadster, 285 pounds; tourer, 299 pounds; four-seater, two-door saloon or two-seater saloonette, 345 pounds; and for a Continental Coupe which, due to rather poor sales, is very rare today, just 350 pounds. Multiply these prices by five for an approximate equivalent in U.S.A. dollars of the mid-thirties, and it's no wonder that even in those days quite a few Americans were inclined to glance longingly at England's sports cars.

In the Relay Race at Brooklands in 1933, a team of two-seater L-types running under M.G. Car Club banners won with an overall average speed of 88.6 mph. The compression ratio of the team cars was raised to 6.8 to 1 and special pistons were fitted. What other "special tuning" these cars had is open to conjecture— well polished ports, complete balancing, and matched rods and pistons, no doubt. The same three L-types ran in the 1933 International Alpine Trials to win their class. A well tuned and superbly driven car ran second to the Type K3 the same year in the 500 Miles race at Brooklands at an average of 92 mph, a remarkable performance for a sports car not designed as a racer but with the obviously necessary fine tuning. Finally, a specially prepared works model performed continuously for twenty-four hours at Montlhery at 80.6 mph and covered 2,000 miles at an average of 80.5 mph.

By the beginning of 1934, the parent Morris Motors people were marketing limited quantities of tourers calculated to hold fanciers of Morris cars who were beginning to look longingly at the marque with the octagon. The new Morris Ten Six Special cost an attractive 230 pounds. While lacking the carefree dash of the L-type M.G. and having a very *non-sporting,* synchromesh gearbox, this Morris Special was the handwriting-on-the-wall that called for a bit more in order to retain some 6-cylinder business for M.G.

As originally named, the first Magna (literally "the great"), the Type F, was larger than the Midgets of the period in both wheelbase and engine size including the number of cylinders. Similarly, because the first of the Type K had a smaller engine placing it between the Magnas and the Midgets, it was called the Magnette, or smaller Magna.

The naming system ran afoul of inevitable development when a replacement for the K-type Magnette was introduced. The new Magnette Type N bowed in with a 1,286 cc. engine which was larger than any of the Magna powerplants. This was the engine also used in the last of the Type K models, the KN as already observed.

Introduced in March, 1934, some 740 Type N models were built with the final unit rolling from the line in November, 1936, the last overhead camshaft M.G. before the war. This Magnette was destined to be the forerunner of another rare competition model.

The *Magna* vs. *Magnette* naming scheme set off further confusion because the chassis of the Type N

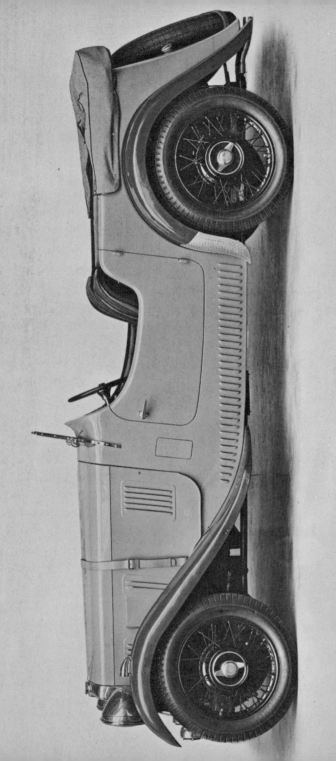

The products of Morris Motors are always of comparative interest to M.G. enthusiasts. In 1934, the Morris Ten Special Six competed in the "light six" market where M.G. was gaining ground. (*The Motor*)

Magnette, with a 96-inch and 45-inch wheelbase and tread respectively, was larger than the previous Magnas. There were other innovations: the traditional M.G. rack-and-pinion steering was livened up with ultra quick steering—just one turn lock-to-lock (Detroit, please notice)—and, for the first time on any M.G., wheels of 18 inches diameter were used. Brakes all around were the familiar 12-inch drums. Because buyers were demanding quieter driving, the bodies were mounted on the chassis with rubber blocks.

Body choices of the times favored two- and four-seaters. Two coach-built bodies were available: an Allingham two-plus-two-seater, open model featuring a smartly sloping rear deck concealing a luggage boot; and a smart, streamlined Airline Coupe made by Carbodies, Ltd., of Coventry. (An Airline Coupe on a Type PA Midget chassis is illustrated in Chapter 3.)

The engine of the N-type featured the KD block of Types K1 and K2 Magnette with the stroke increased 1 mm. for a capacity of 1,286 cc. Dual 1⅛-inch S.U. carburetors, coil ignition, and a 6.1 compression ratio gave 56 bhp at 5,500 rpm. The clutch was a single plate type, built tough, coupled to a 4-speed, non-synchromesh gearbox with the same close ratios used in the Type KN.

Weights were increasing, the two-seater roadster tipping the scales at nearly one ton. Nevertheless, approximately 15.9 mph per 1,000 rpm was available, and *The Autocar,* in the issue of August 24, 1934, reported a road test in which speed was timed at 80.72

The Type N Magnette of 1934 introduced the smallest wheels ever on an M.G. Shown is the four-seater NA tourer. Steering was exceptionally quick. (British Motor Corp.)

The lines of the Type NB are a delight from every angle; there were only detail changes from the NA. (British Motor Corp.)

mph over a half-mile course, and acceleration from zero to 60 mph at 22.8 seconds. Other reports state a top speed of about 83 mph. *The Autocar* listed gas consumption at 24 miles per gallon.

Though not generally known, there were two production models, the NA and NB. The differences were slight: the NA doors were hinged at the rear while those on the NB were front-hinged in the interest (assumed in view of the performance) of *safety fast*. The NB emerged in July, 1935, and was the *first* M.G. to sport a vertically slatted radiator grille. The price, with two-seater body, was 305 pounds, a good buy for a production, 6-cylinder sports car, with overhead camshaft and he-man styling, that could get out and engage in a bit of competition when the spirit moved. Hill climbs and similar trials were the forte of the NA and NB.

When the officials for the Ulster Tourist Trials ruled out blowers for the 1934 event, necessitating the scratching of the K3 Magnette racer as observed in Chapter 2, a Type N, with a special body, dubbed the "NE" was duly prepared. Despite rumors to the contrary through the years, only seven Type NE racers were built. They were specially modified N-types with bigger carburetors, compression ratio increased to 9.8 to 1, and a carefully machined head-to-block fit which eliminated the head gasket. Hotter valve timing, and different gear ratios driven through a two-plate, heavy duty clutch were the other major modifications.

With a pointed-tail body paneled with just enough aluminum sheathing to cover its nakedness, the NE had no doors and the mudguards were the briefest possible cycle types. (If any NC and ND designations existed, they are unknown.)

Thus turned out, the Type NE special racer developed 74.3 bhp at 6,500 rpm. To protect the bearings, a reserve oil tank fed oil to the sump via a float chamber, and to facilitate high speed handling, the steering mechanism was beefed up. Hydraulic shock absorbers on the front axle supplemented the standard friction snubbers.

Without superchargers according to the new rules, six Type NE specials turned up for the Ulster Tourist Trials and, as expected back at the works, an NE came in first, defeating a big Bentley, a pair of Lagondas, and assorted other large, powerful cars. Having previously lapped Brooklands at over 87 mph, the NE must have had a potential around 100 mph or more. This was the major racing event, and the original purpose, of the Type NE.

While production of the "light six" M.G.s was never very great, the experience gained was to serve well for the successful onslaught upon international records.

Not since the last 2½-liter Six 18/80 Mark II of late 1932 had the octagon crest graced a vehicle in the large car class. No doubt the prestige market appealed to the Abingdon designers who thought it timely to top the cake with a thicker frosting while the Midget tribe, increasing by leaps and bounds, paid the way. No doubt Morris Motors, now in control, agreed.

Thus it was that in March, 1936, the most stylish, finest M.G. of all was introduced. This car, a buxom beauty, was the Type SA, but some die-hards refused to recognize the new offering as a genuine M.G.

Here was a heavy, box-section chassis with a wheelbase of 123 inches, a 53⅜-inch tread, an engine with a capacity of 2,288 cc. (later slightly bored to 2,322 cc.), and a total weight ranging from approximately 3,050 to 3,332 pounds.

Such weight and size put the new Type SA into the "lorry" category according to the purists. Also, the works had, from their viewpoint, committed another unpardonable sin: instead of an overhead camshaft valves were operated by pushrods—the first such on any M.G. since "Old No. 1." To displease the purists even more, conventional spring shackles rather than bronze trunnions carried the rear ends of the semi-elliptic springs, and hydraulic shock absorbers were at each corner rather than friction snubbers. Topping all these pointless changes in their favorite marque were *hydraulic* brakes, a proven invention, which Cecil Kimber had always shunned like the plague. Fortunately, a fly-off handbrake was present and the brake shoes were in large 12-inch drums. Otherwise, it is doubtful that the most rabid would have driven the same roads with this latest creation from Abingdon-on-Thames.

For some strange reason never explained, the Type SA was named the 2 Litre. It apparently never occurred to anyone to christen it more accurately—the 2.3 Litre.

The SA's engine had a compression ratio of 6.5 to 1, coil ignition by Lucas and dual 1¼-inch S.U. carburetors sucking air purified of all pollutants by an air cleaner. In the sump, a full-flow filter served 10 quarts of oil. Of the early models, those with the 2,288 cc. engine had a 4-speed non-synchromesh transmission. When the displacement was increased to 2,322 cc., the third and top gears were synchronized. A single-plate clutch was used in both cases and the listed output for each engine was 78.5 bhp at 4,200 rpm. The propeller shaft was of the open type.

Knock-off wire wheels, 18-inchers, were used and three bodies were offered: a drophead coupe by Tickford, a four-seater tourer elegantly made by Charlesworth, and a works-built four-door saloon. Leather upholstered seats, bucket type in front, window sills and facia panels of choice woods, and rich mohair headliners made the interiors works of art comparable with those of the Alvis and Lagonda carriages of the day.

The SA-type was beautifully balanced, had exceptionally high quality, possessed road manners well above the ordinary, and was capable of sustained speeds of 85 to 90 mph. One paid for such elegance, naturally. However, the 10-gallon fuel tank, lacking a reserve, bore watching since consumption was rarely less than 16 miles per gallon, which would have meant around 19 mpg by the 4-quart, American standard.

Deservedly popular in its class, about 700 Type

The Type SA was a large prestige car; shown is the Coupe de Ville by Tickford. (British Motor Corp.)

SAs were built when the exigencies of war phased it out in September, 1939, along with the Type WA which was officially, and accurately, named the 2.6 Litre. About 370 of the Type WA were built. The price of each was around 500 pounds and up. Several of each type were purchased for police use in major cities.

Introduced in August, 1938, the WA had a chassis almost identical to that of the SA. The principal difference was an increased rear tread to 56¾ inches, permitting a wider rear seat. The engine, based on the SA unit, had a larger 73 mm. bore giving a displacement of 2,561 cc. and increasing the power to 95–100 bhp at 4,400 rpm. Gearbox ratios were changed and synchromesh on all but first gear was standard. Saloon and convertible bodies, coachbuilt, were offered. The styling of Types SA and WA was similar, the chief difference—a reference point for enthusiasts—being adjustable louvers on the bonnet sides of the SA while the WA had fixed, vertical louvers. Normal driving produced 16–18 miles per gallon. In proper tune, the SA would reach close to the magic 100 mph figure.

Large and powerful, these were excellent cars in the class in which, actually, M.G. first made its marque famous—all the more surprising that so many M.G. lovers continue to ignore them even to the present time.

Finest of the pre-war M.G. cars was the elegant Type WA 2.6 Litre on a 123-inch wheelbase. (British Motor Corp.)

SPECIFICATIONS

Type and Name	Cylinders	Bore and Stroke (mm.)	Displacement (cc.)	Compression Ratio ($^1/_m$ to 1)	Supercharged	Brake Horsepower @ rpm	Transmission Speeds	Gear Ratios and Alternates (if any)	Rear Axle Ratios and Alternates (if any)	Tires	Wheelbase (inches)	Tread, Front and Rear
F1 Magna F2 Magna F3 Magna	6	57 x 83	1,271	5.7	no	37.2 @ 4,100	4	1.00 1.36 2.00 4.02	4.78	19 x 4.00	94	42
K1 Magnette	6	57 x 71	1,087 KA engine	6.4	no	39 @ 5,500	4 Pre*	1.00 1.36 2.00 3.40	5.78	19 x 4.75	108	48
K1 Magnette	6	57 x 71	1,087 KB engine	6.4	no	41 @ 5,500	4	1.00 1.36 2.14 3.58	5.78	19 x 4.75	108	48
K1 Magnette	6	57 x 83	1,271 KD engine	6.4	no	48.5 @ 5,500	4 Pre	1.00 1.36 2.00 3.40	5.78	19 x 4.75	108	48
K2 Magnette	6	57 x 71	1,087 KB engine	6.4	no	41 @ 5,500	4	1.00 1.36 2.14 3.58	5.78	19 x 4.75	94³⁄₁₆	48
K2 Magnette	6	57 x 83	1,271 KD engine	6.4	no	48.5 @ 5,500	4 Pre	1.00 1.36 2.00 3.40	5.78	19 x 4.75	94³⁄₁₆	48
KN Magnette	6	57 x 84	1,286	6.1	no	56 @ 5,500	4	1.00 1.36 2.32 4.18	5.78	19 x 4.75	108	48

* "Pre" indicates pre-selector transmission.

SPECIFICATIONS

Type and Name	Cylinders	Bore and Stroke (mm.)	Displacement (cc.)	Compression Ratio ($^1/_m$ to 1)	Supercharged	Brake Horsepower @ rpm	Transmission Speeds	Gear Ratios and Alternates (if any)	Rear Axle Ratios and Alternates (if any)	Tires	Wheelbase (inches)	Tread, Front and Rear
L Magna	6	57 x 71	1,087	6.4	no	41 @ 5,500	4	1.00 1.36 2.14 3.58	3.58	19 x 4.50	94³⁄₁₆	42
NA and NB Magnette	6	57 x 84	1,286	6.1	no	56 @ 5,500	4	1.00 1.36 2.32 4.18	5.125 5.375	18 x 4.75	96	45
NE Magnette	6	57 x 84	1,286	9.8	no	74.3 @ 6,500	4	1.00 1.36 2.14 3.58	4.875	18 x 4.75	96	45
SA 2 Litre	6	69 x 102	2,288	6.5	no	78.5 @ 4,200	4	1.00 1.38 2.13 3.76	4.75	18 x 5.50	123	53⅜
(later)		69.5x102	2,322									
WA 2.6 Litre	6	73 x 102	2,561	6.5	no	95–100 @ 4,400	4	1.00 1.418 2.155 3.646	4.78	18 x 5.50	123	53⅜ 56¾

5 The Alphabet Ends with 4-Cylinder 4-Seaters

WITH the Midgets firmly in control of the sports car market and the luxurious Type SA gaining popularity in the large car field, the M.G. Car Company launched an attack upon the market opportunity in between by plugging the gap vacated by the Magna and Magnette.

In April, 1937, about five months after the last of the N-types, the new and heavier Type VA 1½ Litre was introduced, the third new M.G. without an overhead camshaft. Pushrods were the thing and M.G. powerplants had truly come full circle.

The VA chassis, a rather heavy box-section affair with semi-elliptic leaf springs, hydraulically snubbed, solid axles, and 10-inch-diameter Lockheed hydraulic brakes was extremely heavy. The wheelbase was 108 inches like the K1 Magnette; the tread was 50 inches. Minus the body, the VA chassis alone weighed approximately 2,070 pounds—more than most of the complete Magna and Magnette types it was replacing.

Three bodies were available: a 4-door saloon with front and rear doors hinged at the center post, a sporty 2-door tourer, and a coachbuilt, drop-head, four-seater coupe by Tickford. Beautifully crafted, these bodies were on the heavy side and curb weights for the VA ranged from around 2,460 to 2,800 pounds. The tourer was the lightest and the Tickford coupe the heaviest.

The engine specifications are particularly interesting. The dimensions of the 1,548 cc. engine were reminiscent of those that Old No. 1 M.G. had back in 1923. There the resemblance ended, of course. Based upon engines being used in concurrent larger Morris cars, the VA unit had a full-flow oil filter for the 5½ quarts it used, Lucas ignition, dual 1⅜-inch S.U. carburetors, and 6.5 to 1 compression ratio. The output was 55 bhp at 4,400 rpm. The transmission had synchromesh on all but first gear, and 16.3 mph was listed per 1,000 rpm with the 5.22 to 1 rear axle. Acceleration, due to the car's weight, was not sporting; however, under good conditions with adequate space, the VA could attain 80 mph. Good soundproofing, very sturdy construction of the wood-framed body, and excellent, deeply padded, leather upholstery provided quiet motoring in great comfort over long distances.

The styling, very similar to the larger SA and WA

The Type VA 1½ Litre, tourers and saloons, was the M.G. entry in the quality 4-cylinder family car market. (British Motor Corp.)

types, left little to be desired. It was distinguished by sweeping fenders, deeply cut-away doors on the tourer, plenty of polished wood inside, the classic grille and headlights, and large 19-inch, knock-off wire wheels. The saloon and Tickford models had luggage boots and carried the spare wheel in the left front fender. A well-fitted tool case was standard as was a ta-chometer and a full set of instruments.

The VA was certainly one of the prettiest cars any-where at a time when styling in America was ugliness personified. Fairly popular, and esteemed for good handling despite its relative heaviness, about 2,400 VAs were built and sold to buyers who demanded, and got, more than a run-of-the-mill family car before pro-duction at Abingdon was switched to the implements of war in September, 1939.

The Abingdon works resumed production of family cars in 1947 with the Type Y four-seaters which were based on the Type TC. Both four-door saloon and two-door open tourer models were offered in three series: YA, YB, and YT.

The styling closely followed that of the last prewar M.G. family cars. The most obvious styling difference was the invisible stowage of the spare wheel in a separate bin beneath the luggage boot of the saloon. The doors of the saloon were hinged together at the center body pillar on either side. An all-steel, sliding roof panel was standard. Other useful devices were a blind for the rear window and an efficient fog lamp.

The interiors of each model had leather upholstery

The last M.G. cars with traditional lines were the Y-types of 1947 to 1953; styling was like that of the pre-war VA. (Joseph H. Wherry)

A goodly number of the Type Y and YA 1¼ Litre saloons were brought to America; the "sunshine" roof was a popular feature. (Joseph H. Wherry)

which made an immediate and favorable impression on Americans, many of whom bought the Y-type while on early post-war military duty in the United Kingdom. Front seats were individual bucket types, the rear a bench with a central folding armrest and fixed armrests at each end. The instruments were grouped in two large octagonal frames, one being the tachometer, and the polished wood facia (dashboard) had a glovecase fully half the width of the panel.

The chassis differed considerably from the T.C. sports car counterpart in that the wheelbase was 99 inches and the tread, front and rear respectively, was 47⅜ and 50 inches. Independent front wheel suspension by coil springs was introduced on the Type Y; semi-elliptics, shackle mounted, were used in the rear. Hydraulic shock absorbers and brakes were employed, and a four-wheel, built-in hydraulic jacking system, a Smiths product, was standard. The YA saloon and YT tourer had 16-inch disc wheels; the YB saloon, introduced in 1951, had 15-inch wheels and featured an anti-roll bar. The steering, rack-and-pinion, was quick and positive with well under three turns lock-to-lock. A Bluemel adjustable steering wheel added to the comfort.

The engine of the YA saloon was a single S.U. carburetor version of the 1,250 cc. XPAG pushrod engine used in the TC Midget and was rated at 45 bhp at 4,800 rpm. Due to exceptionally sturdy construction, the small sedan weighed 2,240 pounds at the curb. The twin-carburetor version of this famous

The interior of the Type Y 1¼ Litre saloon was remarkably roomy and luxurious for its size. Handling was sporty. (Joseph H. Wherry)

engine, rated at 54.4 bhp at 5,200 rpm, was used in the YB saloon and in all of the YT tourers. Both models had hardwood-framed bodies paneled in heavier steel than was common on American cars.

These were fine automobiles though not spectacular, nor were they intended to be. The author ran a YA model frequently in the early 1950's and had occasion to road test one at the time. The 4-speed transmission, with synchromesh on all but first gear, was butter-smooth and would take the car to a true 30 mph in 6.3 seconds using first gear only. From rest to 60 mph took a flat 29 seconds and because third gear was good for a bit more than 60 mph, there was no need to shift more than twice.

The absolute top speed of the well-worn YA tested was 71 mph. There is no doubt that the more powerful YB and the slightly lighter YT would have turned 75 mph rather easily. These were quiet, comfortable, and remarkably roadable cars with no vices, and the craftsmanship that they exhibited outshone that of many a larger car.

The YA and YB were produced well into 1953, the YT from 1948 to 1950. All told, 8,700 were built— all the factory could turn out. Some were imported into the U.S.A. and were deservedly well liked, many Americans learning from them that small cars could be well built, give a good ride, and hold the road as well as or better than bulky, heavy cars.

Though some are reluctant to admit it, the facilities of the many affiliated manufacturers now a part of the

The post-war Type ZA family saloon revived the Magnette name and also introduced its body-chassis structures to the M.G. line. (Joseph H. Wherry)

The Type ZA and AB Magnette family cars brought envelope-styling to M.G. Many were not happy with the change. (Joseph H. Wherry)

British Motor Corporation do allow some excellent developments to be adapted to the requirements of the various individual works. The purist objects to such broad applications of components, body shells for example, claiming this destroys the thoroughbred qualities of a marque. This attitude is justified to a degree. Nevertheless, since we are now living in an age of mass production, most of us have to live with the situation.

Television viewers will, on occasion, have seen familiar looking sedans driven by police in English movies—Wolseley cars. Before affiliation with B.M.C., the Wolseley factory supplied coachwork for various cars like the Ruxton, a famous American classic of 1929–1932.

The Type Y was the last thoroughbred M.G. family car, but its successor, the Type Z Magnette, was, nevertheless, an excellent vehicle. The unit body and chassis, with slight modifications, was shared with certain Riley and Wolseley models.

The wheelbase on the new Magnette introduced in 1953 was 102 inches and the tread was 51 inches. The full-width body made the new sedan sufficiently wide to accommodate a family of five. The finish was in the M.G. tradition with polished walnut facia-panel and windowsills. Top grade cowhide covered individual front seats and the rear bench. Twin fog lamps were standard and the vertical M.G. grille, now slightly curved, retained a hint of the classic.

Independent front suspension by coil springs and quick rack-and-pinion gave fine steering with 2¾ turns

The interior of Type Z Magnettes upheld M.G. tradition for leather and polished wood facias. The half-octagon hood over the speedometer, the huge glovecase, and clock above the windshield suggest the fine craftsmanship of this model. (Joseph H. Wherry)

lock-to-lock. The rear suspension, by semi-elliptic springs, was not independent. Hydraulic brakes and shock absorbers completed the running gear. Synchromesh on the top three speeds—a "Manumatic" clutch was optional—teamed with a pushrod-operated, overhead-valve engine displacing 1,489 cc. provided good performance due to well chosen gear ratios. The car weighed approximately 2,500 pounds.

There were two models. The ZA engine's compres-

The Type ZB Magnette had more power and introduced the "Vari-tone" color schemes. (British Motor Corp.)

sion ratio was a moderate 7.15 to 1 and the output was 60 bhp at 4,600 rpm. In 1956, the demand for more power resulted in the ZB type with a slight styling facelift and compression ratio increased to 8.3 to 1 with a resulting output of 68 bhp at 5,500 rpm. Both models employed dual downdraft S.U. carburetors.

The author road tested the ZA and ZB with the following results in brief:

	Type ZA	*Type ZB*
Zero to 30 mph	7.2 sec.	6.3 sec.
Zero to 45 mph	13.3 sec.	11.8 sec.
Zero to 60 mph	22.8 sec.	20.5 sec.
Maximum speed	81 mph	84 mph
Fuel consumption	25 mpg (U.S.)	28–30 mpg

Comfortable, tough, and exceptionally easy to handle, the Magnette was a shock to many M.G. buffs. It was a very good car. About 36,000 were built before being phased out in mid-1958.

SPECIFICATIONS

Type and Name	Cylinders	Bore and Stroke (mm.)	Displacement (cc.)	Compression Ratio ($^1/_m$ to 1)	Supercharged	Brake Horsepower @ rpm	Transmission Speeds	Gear Ratios and Alternates (if any)	Rear Axle Ratios and Alternates (if any)	Tires	Wheelbase (inches)	Tread, Front and Rear
VA 1½ Litre	4	69.5 x 102	1,548	6.5	no	55 @ 4,400	4	1.00 1.35 1.95 3.38	5.22	19 x 5.00	108	50
YA 1¼ Litre	4	66.5 x 90	1,250	7.2	no	45 @ 4,800	4	1.00 1.385 2.07 3.50	5.143	16 x 5.25	99	47⅜ 50
YB 1¼ Litre	4	66.5 x 90	1,250	7.4	no	48 @ 4,800	4	1.00 1.355 2.07 3.50	5.143	15 x 5.50	99	47⅜ 50
YT 1¼ Litre	4	66.5 x 90	1,250	7.2	no	54.4 @ 5,200	4	1.00 1.355 2.07 3.50	5.143	16 x 5.25	99	47⅜ 50
ZA Magnette	4	73 x 88.9	1,489	7.15	no	60 @ 4,600	4	1.00 1.374 2.214 3.64	4.875	15 x 5.50	102	51
ZB Magnette	4	73 x 88.9	1,489	8.3	no	68 @ 5,500	4	1.00 1.374 2.214 3.64	4.55	15 x 5.50	102	51

6 The Record-breaking Experimentals

THE EX120 had done its assigned task well as a proto-type and as a means of getting M.G. into the business of record-breaking. To go after records systematically, however, Kimber decided to create a car for the specific purpose of smashing every existing International Class H mark. Such a vehicle, the EX127, was completed late in the summer of 1931. The new-record car was based generally upon the EX120 and was, as events proved, appropriately dubbed the "Magic Midget."

The rear axle differential was well off-center near the left wheel. To keep the driver and the engine reasonably centered, the transmission and propeller shaft, and the engine itself with its supercharger drive, were offset 7 degrees from the center line. The driver sat beside the propeller shaft with the seat of his pants barely 6 inches from the roadway.

Very early in October, 1931, the crew readied the EX-127 at Montlhery, and consulting engineer Ernest Eldridge, even more generously proportioned than Eyston, squeezed himself into the car. Years before, Eldridge had lost the sight of one eye, a handicap in high-speed driving. Nevertheless, Eldridge got off, opened up the Magic Midget, and broke the 5-kilometer record at 110.28 mph, a courageous feat. In December, Eyston arrived at Montlhery, defied the ice, and cracked four records at 114 mph.

The two-mile-a-minute goal spurred on the entire company and in February, 1932, Kimber and his men were on the smooth seashore near Pendine in Wales. A new type of three-piece windshield, steeply raked and with a curious, horizontal, open slit, had been devised after consultations with aerodynamicists on the problem of obscured vision due to seashore spray and mist at high speeds. The full belly pan was modified, and all external bolts and rivets were ingeniously streamlined.

The sands were smooth but the tides were bothersome, and despite stop watches indicating that Eyston had topped 120 mph by a safe margin, the efforts came a cropper and the average computed speed was 118.39 mph. This was a world record for a 750 cc. car but short of the 120 mph goal. In a mood as dismal as the weather, the car and the crew left the wintry Welsh coast.

In December, 1932, Eyston and company returned to Montlhery with the EX127 and quickly broke the Fly-

EX127, the "Magic Midget," driven by Capt. George Eyston achieved two miles a minute at Montlhery in 1932. Here Eyston gets a start. (British Motor Corp.)

ing Kilometre and Flying Mile records at 120.56 mph and all the others up to 10 kilos. The target was shattered. There followed a stint by Eyston on a specially groomed J3 with which he broke the 24-hour and 2,000-kilometer records at more than 70 mph.

Then Eyston co-driving with another famed man, Denly, put in another 24 hours on the EX127. The net was an average of 86.67 mph and the complete conquest of Class H records for M.G. in a hair-raising series of actions which would make a classic film of those incomparable men in their Midget speedsters. Christmas, 1932, was a happy one at the works.

Later, after a complete overhaul at Abingdon, Denly drove the EX127, with a new and even slimmer body too scant for Eyston, at Montlhery to new Flying Mile and Kilometre records at 128.6 mph. Then EX127 was purchased by Bobby Kohlrausch, a German driver of note, who broke the Flying Mile record with over 130 mph in Hungary in 1935. Kohlrausch then had a bronze cylinder head made in Germany which brought the brake horsepower up to 146 at 7,500 rpm with supercharger running at high pressure. Kohlrausch next raised the Flying Mile at Frankfurt in 1936 to 140.6 mph after which the EX127 became the object of technical interest to German engineers. The Magic Midget never returned to England.

Record breaking was becoming a pleasant M.G. habit so when George Eyston ordered a car with which to assault Class G records, Kimber was delighted. Using a K3 engine with a Powerplus supercharger and an underslung frame similar to that of the K3 but with box-section longerons rather than channels, the new EX135 was actually a development of the famed Magnette racer. The power train was angularly offset 6 degrees and the driver's seat was sandwiched between the propeller shaft and the frame side.

The story of the fabrication of the EX135 was as full of humorous incidents as of technical problems. It was literally necessary to design the tiny record car around the owner. Eyston, consequently, came to the works for frequent "fittings" as it is so aptly put by John Thornley in his book, *Maintaining the Breed*. In fact, Thornley's account of the amazing career of EX135 is so extensive, and so often amusing, that those interested are urged to read it. Space permits only a brief discussion of the car, nicknamed "Humbug" because of its striped paint job in the official cream and brown M.G. colors.

In 1934, with Eyston driving, the EX135 broke the Class G records for the Flying Mile and Kilometre at 128.7 mph, the Ten Mile record at 128.5 mph, the One Hour record with 120.88 miles, and other Class G records for a total of twelve. Then in 1935 when the ban was placed against M.G. works-sponsored competition, Eyston sold the car to a businessman.

In the autumn of 1937, Cecil Kimber and Lt. Col. Goldie Gardner put their heads together. The latter had been setting records with a K3 Magnette—the Flying Mile at more than 148 mph for instance—and he and Kimber decided that old EX135 Humbug with a completely enclosed body might attain 170 mph in Class G.

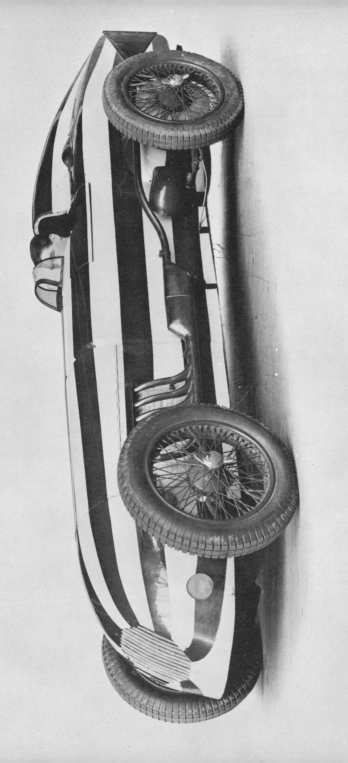

In the brown and cream stripes that gave EX135 its nickname of "Humbug," the experimental speedster is shown in the 1934 form in which it won twelve Class G International records. (British Motor Corp.)

Gardner acquired the EX135 and it was rebuilt at the works and fitted with an extremely low body. The driver had to lie on his back in a hammock-like seat to decrease overall height.

On November 9, 1938, Kimber, Gardner and the fully streamlined EX135 were ready on a stretch of the German Autobahn near Frankfurt. In two-way runs, flat out, Gardner attained an average of 187.6 mph, a new Class G record and 17 mph more than had been hoped for. In spring, 1939, the EX135 assault team was once again on the Autobahn near Dessau. The engine had been modified upward into Class F, and Gardner captured the Flying Mile and Kilometre records with 203 mph.

After the war, Gardner had EX135 rebuilt again and the engine modified so that the number of operating cylinders could be quickly changed. For record runs in Class H in 1946, the EX135 ran on all six cylinders. In 1947, the car ran on four cylinders and in 1949 on just three cylinders in Class I. In 1950, all but two cylinders were blocked off and records fell to the fabulous M.G. in the 500 cc. Class J.

By 1951, such efforts were designated B.M.C. Development Projects. A supercharged Type TD engine was installed. Gardner and the veteran EX135 went to the Utah salt flats where more records fell in Class F. Still other records were broken in Class F and in Class E with the car powered by a 2-liter Jaguar engine in 1952. The following year saw the retirement of 64-year-old Lt. Col. A.T.G. Goldie Gardner and the 18-

With a streamlined body, EX135 was driven by Lt. Col. Goldie Gardner at over 200 miles per hour on the Utah salt flats in 1952. (British Motor Corp.)

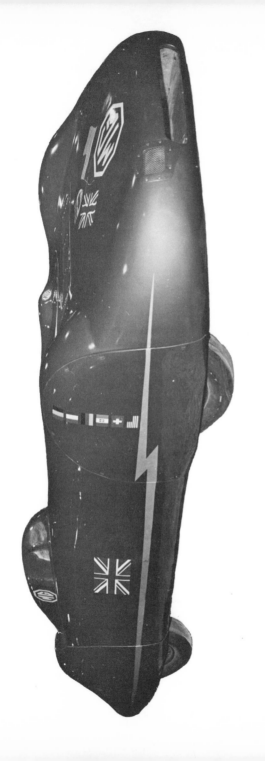

In the autumn of 1951 the EX135 was exhibited in the Autorama in Los Angeles. The scenes of triumphs are depicted by the flags of Belgium, France, Italy, the Netherlands, Switzerland, the United States, and the United Kingdom. (Joseph H. Wherry)

year-old EX135. Together they had swept five of the
ten International Classes with the greatest speeds ever
attained.

To Americans, the records set by the EX135 in Utah
are of special interest:

August 20, 1951, Class F	50 kilos	127.8 mph
(with M.G. TD engine)	50 miles	130.6 mph
	100 kilos	132.0 mph
	100 miles	135.1 mph
	200 kilos	136.6 mph
	1 hour	137.4 mph
August 18, 1952, Class E	50 kilos	143.2 mph
(with 2-liter Jaguar	50 miles	147.4 mph
engine)	100 kilos	148.7 mph
August 20, 1952, Class F	5 miles	189.5 mph
(with M.G. TD engine)	10 kilos	182.8 mph

The year after Goldie Gardner retired, George Eyston was again piloting an M.G. record car, the EX179.
The body had lines similar to those of the EX135 with
suspension including many Type TF components and
one or two Type VA parts. Coil springs were used in the
front, semi-elliptics aft, all snubbed down tightly and
controlled by friction shock absorbers.

Several special engines based upon the TF powerplant, and using fuels even more exotic than those used
by previous M.G. record cars, were developed.

The sprint engine developed 97.5 bhp at 6,500 rpm
while the less highly-tuned endurance engine developed
81 bhp at 5,500 rpm. Compression ratios ran as high
as 11.8 to 1. These were relatively simple, overhead-
valve, pushrod engines that were *not* supercharged.

On the Bonneville Salt Flats for long-distance records, Eyston's co-driver was Ken Miles, well known to the M.G. world as a top sports car competitor. When the 12-hour ordeal was finished, the EX179 had garnered wide publicity for M.G. by taking seven International Class F records plus some twenty-five American records with speeds consistently around 120 mph.

With the higher powered sprint engine installed and Miles in the cockpit, the EX179 was pushed off. The mean of the resulting 10-mile, two-way runs was a Class F record-shattering 153.69 mph.

In 1956, fitted with a new twin-overhead-camshaft engine, and supercharged, the EX179 took sixteen Class F records, and in 1957, with a prototype engine, the successor to the EX135 added nine major Class G records to its list, running both with and without a blower.

These successes did not conclude M.G.'s record-breaking. In 1957, the works *équipe* was back on the Utah sands with the EX181, a rear-engined car powered with another prototype of the M.G.A twin-overhead-camshaft engine fitted with a monstrous Shorrock supercharger. On the 27th of August, Stirling Moss captured five records in Class F with speeds timed as high as 245.6 mph. Two years later, Phil Hill piloted the EX181, with the engine bored out, over the Bonneville sands to break six more records in Class E with a top recorded speed of 254.9 mph.

Truly, M.G. had come a long way since that first Experimental, the EX120, smashed those first notable records for the Abingdon works at Montlhery.

Powered by a rear engine, the EX181 was driven by Phil Hill to six records and 254.9 miles per hour on the Bonneville flats in 1959. (British Motor Corp.)

7 Post-war Midgets and the "New Look"

AT the end of World War II, the pent-up need for cars of all kinds, including sports cars, and the drain on resources caused by the war, precluded the development of new models. The decision was wisely made, therefore, to continue producing the pre-war Midgets.

The Type TC Midget was the welcome result. This ever popular model was introduced late in 1945 in the two-seater sports version, and was based upon the pre-war TB. Close examination was necessary to spot the few changes. The box-section frame was already excellent, and the XPAG engine with overhead valves operated by pushrods was retained with minor refinements only: twin S.U. $1\frac{1}{4}$-inch-diameter carburetors replaced the former 1-inch duals, and the compression ratio was slightly reduced to 7.25 to 1. The output remained the same, 54.4 bhp at 5,200 rpm. The body was made about 4 inches wider without changing the tread or wheelbase and the seats were roomier. All the traditional instruments in circular dials were on the wood facia. The new Midget still hugged the ground on 19-inch wire wheels, but the rear ends of the leaf springs were slung by shackles instead of sliding trunnions.

When the first TC Midgets were exported to America—a sports car desert—they were an immediate sensation. Motorists, starved for automotive fun, found a

The Type TC Midget defines sports cars to enthusiasts everywhere. (Joseph H. Wherry)

This beautifully maintained TC is regularly driven by owner Gert Orla Jensen. (Joseph H. Wherry)

The starboard side of the engine shows the traditional Skinners Union carburetors on the Type TC. (Joseph H. Wherry)

two-seater that would achieve 80 mph while holding the road better than anything that Detroit was turning out, deliver around 25 miles per 4-quart gallon, and accelerate from a standing start to 60 mph in 22 seconds. America learned that a car weighing a scant 1,800 pounds could hold the road, handle beautifully, and give a lot of driving enjoyment. With the simple cam steering, the quick one-and-one-half turns lock-to-lock made parking easy. American cars of those years could not claim that they were fun to drive.

The magnificently kept engine of Mr. Gert Orla Jensen's TC Midget from the left side. (Joseph H. Wherry)

For the first time in America, the TC brought sports car racing to the men of modest means. Already well established in England, branches of the M.G. Car Club sprouted all over the United States and thrived. Weekend race meetings and trials attracted owner-drivers by the hundreds. The M.G. TC, more than any other marque, gave birth to the Sports Car Club of America and "sports car" became a household term. TC Midgets were modified with compression ratios as high as 11 to 1, specialty shops provided camshafts and other "special tuning" equipment, and owners became their own mechanics.

By the time the TC gave way to a new model in 1949, roughly 10,000 had been built and sold, well over half of them in the United States where sports cars had come to stay.

The Type TD Midget continued the traditional lines but added re-styled fenders, 15-inch disc wheels, and an

The facia of the Type TC continued the pre-war design. (British Motor Corp.)

By 1951 the M.G. Car Club was well established on the West Coast. Here Mr. Dick Hayward of the Long Beach chapter and the author discuss sports cars during an auto show. (Author's archives)

D. F. Marsh rounds a corner in his TC Midget during a race at the Cumberland, Maryland, airport in 1953. (Joseph H. Wherry)

William A. Eager III blasts his modified TC Midget up Mount Equinox in New Hampshire during a 1953 hill climb. (Joseph H. Wherry)

This nicely restored TD Midget is owned by Mr. Richard Negley. (Joseph H. Wherry)

Instruments of the TD are arranged for efficiency, one of the hall-marks of a true sports car. (British Motor Corp.)

overall length of 145 inches making it a half a foot longer. The seating, also, was a couple of inches wider and the behind-the-seat luggage boot was slightly more generous. The body of sheet metal over the traditional seasoned hardwood frame was squared off in the back and the wedge-shaped fuel tank and spare wheel were in the best sporting tradition. The wood facia gave way to a leatherette-covered dash containing a large glove-case, and the instrument layout was changed. Purists were appalled as they had been in years past.

The independent front suspension of the TD Midget contrasts with the individual styling changes on wings and bonnet made by one owner. (Joseph H. Wherry)

The TD, however, repeated the success of previous models and about 30,000 were built and sold, nearly 20,000 of them in America, by the time of model change-over in 1953.

Two features of the Type Y saloon, elsewhere detailed, were incorporated in the TD: the excellent, independent front suspension by unequal A-frames and coil springs, and rack-and-pinion steering. The former gave a better ride while the latter made for lighter steering; wheel turns lock-to-lock were a bit slower but still well under three turns. The frame was of box-section longerons (*not* the first for M.G. as many have believed) but a casual glance might mislead one into thinking channel steel was used, the inner box-facings being slightly inset. The wheelbase was not changed but the tread was increased. The XPAG engines and transmissions were continued without change in output.

Owners raced and rallied with the TD, engaged in gymkhanas and hill climbs. Though about one hundred pounds heavier than the TC, a well maintained TD had a nearly identical performance.

The cry for more power prompted Abingdon to produce the TDC, officially named the Type TD Mark II, in 1950. Optional wire wheels offered a change in appearance, but the changes of real import were in the engine. The compression ratio was raised to 8.0 to 1, all the ports and combustion chambers were polished, and larger 36 mm. inlet and 34 mm. exhaust valves were fitted together with heavier valve springs. Camshaft changes were commensurate. Larger 1½-inch-diameter

A TD Midget's frame ready for the body to be installed. (Joseph H. Wherry)

H. W. Wilson, Jr., in his TD Midget number 83 leads the pack round a curve at Cumberland, Maryland, in the 1953 race. (Joseph H. Wherry)

R. J. McKinsey's much modified TD Midget was a familiar sight in races during the mid-fifties. (Joseph H. Wherry)

S.U. carburetors and bigger air cleaners were also standard on the TD Mark II as was higher-capacity Lucas ignition equipment. The output was, therefore, increased to an eventual 60 bhp at 5,500 rpm.

To firm up the suspension for better cornering while racing, Andrex friction shock absorbers were added front and rear to supplement the Armstrong or Girling hydraulic snubbers. All of this increased the weight, a Mark II TD weighing 2,015 pounds at the curb. The performance was increased with improved acceleration and a maximum speed of about 85 mph.

A "competition kit" was offered enabling TD owners to bring their cars up to TD Mark II standards for class competition.

Americans, taking a back seat to no one in modifying production cars, changed Type TD and the Mark II to suit their fancy and many were built up to top 100 mph.

Altering the TD Midget did not remain the province of competition drivers alone. Inskip Motors, distributors, of New York City, lengthened the frame of a TD making it a four-seater. Displayed glamorously in the 1953 International Motor Show alongside a Rolls Royce limousine in New York City, this special TD Tourer was offered at $2,900.

An even more ambitious M.G. program was embarked upon by S. H. Arnolt, Inc., of Chicago during 1953– 1954. On a standard TD Mark II chassis, Arnolt installed luxurious four-seater Italian coachwork. The performance with about two hundred pounds of additional weight was not quite up to Mark II standards, but with

Inskip Motors displayed this custom-built Type TD Midget four-seater tourer at the New York International Motor Show in 1953. (Joseph H. Wherry)

Italian-built *grand tourismo* bodies graced TD Midget chassis as offered by the S. H. Arnolt Company in Chicago. (Joseph H. Wherry)

The lines of the TF Midget blended traditional and modern styling elements. (British Motor Corp.)

wire wheels and faithful adherence to basic M.G. lines, the Arnolt M.G. was a lovely car with a price to match —around $4,000. Nevertheless, the sports car gospel was spreading like wildfire and several dozen Arnolt M.G.s were produced. A rare closed variant, this car is still outstanding.

In the early autumn of 1953, the last model of the Type T Midgets was introduced, the TF. Though an excellent car, the TF disappointed many to whom it was a rather unhappy effort to wed traditional styling to modern lines. The net result of the facelift was a steeply slanted, slightly curved grille, headlights grafted to the fenders, and overall length slightly increased to 147 inches.

The TF Midget was a styling development only, the improvements to the engine in the TD Mark II being retained, as was independent front suspension. Disc wheels were standard; knock-off wire wheels were optional.

The interior of the TF was considerably changed: the seats became individual, and the dash was radically redesigned with the instruments in the center flanked by a large, open parcel compartment on each side. The windshield wipers were relocated to the bottom but the screen still folded flat for racing.

The appeals to Abingdon for even more power were heard, and in July, 1954, the TF 1500 was introduced. Though the stroke of the engine remained the same, the bore was increased considerably from 66.5 to 72 mm. In effect, due to improved foundry techniques, the

The instruments of the TF Midget were steeply angled and centered. (British Motor Corp.)

1,466 cc. XPEG engine of the TF 1500 was an entirely new unit. Compared with the TF, the output of 63 bhp at 5,500 rpm was a respectable increase. The torque of 76 foot-pounds at 3,000 rpm, considerably better than the 64 foot-pounds at 5,200 rpm of the TD Mark II and the TF, enabled the TF 1500 to accelerate much more quickly.

In production until early in 1955, somewhat more than 9,600 Type TF and TF 1500 Midgets were built. Many believed that the softened suspension was an illogical concession to mass mores, and the styling offended others, but in reality the TF 1500 was in many ways a superior car though outclassed in competition

A small bonnet plaque identifies the more powerful TF 1500 Midget. (Joseph H. Wherry)

Mr. G. M. Gardner restored this TF 1500 Midget to perfection. (Joseph H. Wherry)

by several continental marques. Finally modern times, the all-steel envelope body, and other factors overwhelmed this last of the M.G. "traditionals."

For several months in mid-1955 no sports car was produced at Abingdon. Then in September the most revolutionary M.G. in twenty years was introduced— the M.G.A—an almost complete break with the past. The second time around the alphabet, the new M.G.A was not even called a Midget although the wheelbase was the same as that of the last several Midget types, and the tread was nearly identical.

Though a radical departure from anything that had ever come out of Abingdon, the M.G.A came by its "new look" honestly. George Phillips, a successful sports car racer, had done rather well on his privately entered M.G. TC Special in the 1950 Le Mans race, gaining second place in his class. Accordingly, the works consented to build him a streamlined TD Special for the 1951 event. Phillips didn't win his class in 1951 with the TD Special due to a variety of circumstances. However, the exceptional performance of his car was a clear indication that a streamlined envelope body would pay off.

The designer of Phillips' TD Special was Sydney Enever and what he had come up with inspired him to improve the streamlined TD even more. To decrease the overall height, Enever splayed the longitudinal chassis members outward allowing the seats to be placed lower inside the rails. (The frame of the EX179 was nearly identical.) The result was an experimental

Production of the M.G.A surpassed all other models of the marque. Shown: M.G.A "Twin Cam." (British Motor Corp.)

named the EX175. Further development resulted in the EX182 with lightweight aluminum bodies for racing.

The engine was the B.M.C. "B series" unit displacing 1,489 cc. Relatively easy to produce and already serving well in the Type Z Magnette saloon, several engines were given the "tuning" treatment: special camshafts, 9.4 to 1 compression-ratio heads with inlet ports arranged so that special carburetors could be placed on either side for heating by the exhaust manifold if desired, and the like. The output thus developed was in excess of 80 bhp at 5,500 rpm. The goal was a team of cars in the Le Mans race on June 11, 1955. This was the first time in twenty years that the works had officially engaged in competition.

As things turned out, this event was a scene of stark tragedy, a Mercedes-Benz crashing out of control and causing widespread death and havoc and near cancellation of the race. Out of sixty cars at the start, only a third remained to complete the twenty-four hours. Two of the M.G. Specials came through with 248 and 230 laps at 86.2 and 82 mph respectively for a "technical success" as John Thornley described the affair in *Maintaining the Breed*. These were the racing prototypes of the all-new M.G. introduced three months later. A new name as well as Type designation—M.G.A—for a new start.

The works was getting set to produce the model which looked almost exactly like the Le Mans cars. The all-steel body concealed a 1,489 cc. "B series" engine in virtually the same tune as its mate in the Type ZB Magnette saloon. The moderate 8.3 to 1 compression ratio and 1½-inch S.U. dual carburetors made maintenance simple, yet a top speed of 95 mph was on tap for sports car fans who wanted a production Class F car with high performance.

The frame consisted of very rigid box-sections swept outward 45½ inches wide at the cockpit allowing the seats to be low as on the EX182. The independent, coil-spring, front suspension was based upon that of the TF Midget, the rear axle and brake system followed those of the Type Z Magnette. Rack-and-pinion steering gave positive and light control with 2¾ turns lock-to-lock and virtually no high-mileage wear as owners have learned. Inside, the bucket seats and a sporty facia provided exceptional comfort; behind was a spacious luggage boot.

Improved valve-timing and carburetion increased the power to 68 bhp at 5,500 rpm and finally on later models to 72 bhp without increasing engine speed. On this version—there was no model designation change other than to identify the engine as type 15GD—the synchromesh transmission was improved and the propeller shaft strengthened.

From April, 1959, to April, 1960, the high-performance and sometimes cantankerous M.G.A Twin Cam model was produced, about 2,000 of them, for the serious racing devotee. The engine had an increased bore, a displacement of 1,588 cc., and with dual overhead camshafts, dual 1¾-inch S.U. carburetors, and compres-

The dual overhead camshaft engine made the M.G.A "Twin Cam" model a 115-miles-an-hour car. (British Motor Corp.)

sion ratio of 9.9 to 1, the timing was critical. It required the sort of understanding and attention that only the most rabid enthusiast is able to muster. This model with 108 bhp at 6,700 rpm was a superb performer. Four-wheel Dunlop disc brakes and center-locking disc wheels with vent holes were standard, the brakes equating safety with high performance. The entire suspension system was tightened up for this limited-production competition car which turned in speeds of 115 mph with ease and accelerated to 60 mph in less than 10 seconds.

The M.G.A-1600 was introduced in May, 1959, and remained in production almost two years. The engine was a pushrod version of the 1,588 cc. unit used in the Twin Cam model and gave high performance with fine handling aided by Lockheed disc brakes on the front wheels. With 80 bhp at 5,600 rpm, the A-1600 was a 100-mph sports car that did not require, in general, more than normal common-sense maintenance.

The official designations of the variants of the M.G.A became a bit involved with the A-1600 Mark II which was introduced in April, 1961. In production fourteen months until June, 1962, the Mark II had an almost entirely new 1,622 cc. engine—the largest in any M.G. since the war—in which the specified 89 mm. bore was about the only familiar feature. The body was improved structurally although the appearance did not change. Brackets for seat belts were built in rather than added on, and alterations in the drive-line, principally in the rear axle, improved performance with a maximum of 105 mph. The compression ratio, increased to 8.9 to 1, required premium-grade fuel at all times. The A-1600 Mark II developed 93 bhp at 5,500 rpm.

For the American market, where owners were subjecting their M.G.s to transcontinental trips and distances unknown in England, oil coolers were standard. The works also recommended steel-disc, bolted-on wheels because of their greater strength. Fashion, how-

Coupe as well as roadster bodies were offered on all M.G.A variants. (British Motor Corp.)

The M.G.A. 1600 was identical in appearance to the earlier M.G.A. (British Motor Corp.)

ever, demanded knock-off wire wheels and they were available on all models.

When M.G.A production ceased in June, 1962, nearly 101,000 had been built, of which around two-thirds were purchased by eager buyers in the U.S.A.

Despite the overwhelming acceptance of the M.G.A, a gap remained, technically and sentimentally, in the M.G. line. There had to be another M.G. Midget. To fill this need created by the absence of an M.G. sports car in the $2,000 price bracket, Abingdon introduced a new and ultra-modern Midget in June, 1961. Admittedly inspired by the B.M.C.-related Austin-Healey Sprite, the new Midget was the successor in the long line of sports cars built for the average man with limited means.

If the M.G.A was an almost total break with tradition, the Midget Mark I, as it has been officially named, was a complete departure. Instead of the usual separate frame, a unitized or integral structure was used. Extremely rigid and virtually rattle-free for life, this all-welded frame-body was powered initially with the 948 cc. B.M.C. "A series" engine. With its 8.3 to 1 compression ratio and dual 1¼-inch S.U. carburetors, the output was 46.4 bhp at 5,500 rpm. The transmission had four speeds, synchronized on the top three, and the propeller shaft was open.

Soon after introduction, an alternate cylinder head with 9.1 to 1 compression ratio was offered, giving 50 bhp without affecting engine speed.

Though the unitized Midget Mark I was revolution-

The Midget Mark I had a unit body and frame; it was the last of the roadster Midgets. (British Motor Corp.)

ary in structure, it was a throwback to the Midgets of early years with its wheelbase of 80 inches and front tread of 45¾ inches. Overall length was 136 inches, 20 inches shorter than the M.G.A. Total weight was around 1,550 pounds. Nicely streamlined, the styling had forsaken the classic vertical grille, the M.G. trademark since late 1926. The octagon medallion remained on the grille and steering wheel. Beneath the rear deck were 11 cubic feet of luggage space. Combined with an exceptionally comfortable cockpit with foam-filled leatherette, individual bucket seats, these features made the new Midget a fine 80-mile-an-hour sports or cross-country machine. Easily attached side curtains were standard and a detachable hardtop was a popular option.

Quick rack-and-pinion steering with independent front suspension by coil springs and rather short, quarter-elliptic, rear leaf springs gave precise handling with roadability leaving little to be desired.

When the 1962 London Motor Show opened in October, the Midget exhibit displayed an improved engine with increases in bore and stroke. Basically like the Morris Minor engine, displacement was 1,098 cc. Fitted with an 8.9 to 1 compression head, the bhp was 55 at 5,500 rpm, enough of an increase to produce about 85 mph without increasing engine speed. There was no change in model designation. The improved Midget Mark I looked the same but disc brakes in front plus wire wheels gave the enthusiasts what they were asking for.

The Midget Mark I, the final step by Abingdon into the realm of the New Look in cars, remained in production until late in 1964. All told, 26,000 were built, a good start in the fourth decade of the Midget.

SPECIFICATIONS

Type and Name	Cylinders	Bore and Stroke (mm.)	Displacement (cc.)	Compression Ratio (1/m to 1)	Brake Horsepower @ rpm	Transmission Speeds	Gear Ratios and Alternates (if any)	Rear Axle Ratios and Alternates (if any)	Tires	Wheelbase (inches)	Tread, Front and Rear
TC Midget	4	66.5 x 90	1,250	7.25	54.4 @ 5,200	4	1.00 1.35 1.95 3.38	5.125	19 x 4.50	94	45
TD Midget	4	66.5 x 90	1,250	7.25	54.4 @ 5,200	4	1.00 or 1.385 2.07 3.50	5.125 or 4.875 4.555	15 x 5.50	94	47⅜ 50
TDC Midget Mark II	4	66.5 x 90	1,250	8.0	57 @ 5,500 and 60 @ 5,500	4	1.00 1.385 2.07 3.50	5.125 or 4.875 4.555	15 x 5.50	94	47⅜ 50 wire: 48¾₆ 50¹³⁄₁₆
TF Midget	4	66.5 x 90	1,250	8.0	57 @ 5,500	4	1.00 1.355 2.07 3.50	4.875 or 5.125 4.55	15 x 5.50	94	Same as TD Mark II
TF1500 Midget	4	72 x 90	1,466	8.0	63 @ 5,500	4	1.00 1.355 2.07 3.50	4.875 or 5.125 4.55	15 x 5.50	94	Same as TD Mark II

SPECIFICATIONS

Type and Name	Cylinders	Bore and Stroke (mm.)	Displacement (cc.)	Compression Ratio ($^1/_m$ to 1)	Brake Horsepower @ rpm	Transmission Speeds	Gear Ratios and Alternates (if any)	Rear Axle Ratios and Alternates (if any)	Tires	Wheelbase (inches)	Tread, Front and Rear
A	4	73 x 89	1,489	8.3	68 @ 5,500 later: 72 @ 5,500	4	1.00 1.374 2.214 3.64	4.3	15 x 5.60	94	47⅜ 49
A Twin Cam	4	75.4 x 89	1,588	9.9	108 @ 6,700	4	1.00 1.374 2.214 3.64	4.3	15 x 5.90	94	47⅜ 49
A-1600	4	75.4 x 89	1,588	8.3	80 @ 5,600	4	1.00 1.374 2.214 3.64	4.3	15 x 5.60	94	47⅜ 49
A-1600 Mark II	4	76.2 x 89	1,622	8.9	93 @ 5,500	4	1.00 1.374 2.214 3.64	4.10	15 x 5.60	94	47⅜ 49
Midget Mark I	4	62.9 x 76.2	948	8.3 9.1	46.4 @ 5,500 50 @ 5,500	4			13 x 5.20	80	45¾ 44¾
Midget Mark 1 (after Oct. '62)	4	64.6 x 83.7	1,098	8.9	55 @ 5,500	4	1.00 1.357 1.916 3.200	4.22	13 x 5.20	80	45¾ 44¾

8 M.G.s Today

FOUR distinct models comprise the M.G. line as this is being written: the Magnette family sedan, the 1100 sports sedan, the M.G.B in two body styles, and the Mark II Midget. All but the first are actively marketed in the United States; all four are popular in Canada.

The first of the current models, in chronological order, is the Magnette, introduced in Mark III form in autumn, 1959. The engine, in specifications, dual 1½-inch S.U. carburetors and all, was identical to the powerplant in the Type ZB Magnette.

Mention of the latter justifies explanation for the Mark III designation. In pure conjecture as to why Abingdon did not continue its alphabetical line, it appears that the "Z" end of the alphabet would necessitate coming full circle because the new Magnette was

179

really a different car. Or, since the name "Magnette" was becoming re-established, it could have been considered that the ZA and ZB were Mark I and Mark II, making the new car Mark III.

At any rate, the Mark III Magnette had an all new B.M.C. chassis which with body made it 9 inches longer, at 178 inches overall, than its Type Z predecessor. The overall width and height of 63 and 58⅞ inches were virtually unchanged. However, the completely restyled, unitized structure's wheelbase was, oddly, nearly 3 inches shorter.

The new body-frame unit was shared, with grille and trim differences, with the Morris Oxford and certain of the Wolseley, Riley, and Austin sedans. The engine in the Mark III was like that in the M.G.A. To complete the picture, Austin had merged with the Nuffield Organization back in 1952 to form the British Motor Corporation.

The performance of the Magnette Mark III was nearly identical to that of the Type ZB Magnette already detailed in Chapter 5. At the curb, it weighed 2,500 pounds. The suspension was not changed and the steering was by cam and lever. Inside, a family of five could be rather luxuriously comfortable on genuine leather. The front seats were individual semi-buckets. There was adequate luggage space and walnut trim was used functionally.

In October, 1961, the Mark IV Magnette was introduced. The styling remained the same, but a de-tuned version of the 1,622 cc. engine used in the M.G.A 1600

The family size Magnette Mark III and Mark IV were the first of the current M.G. line to reach production. (British Motor Corp.)

The 1960 Morris Oxford shares unit-body-frame stampings with the Magnette Mark III and IV, a full-circle return to the early days of each marque. (Joseph H. Wherry)

Mark II sports car was used. This change necessitated a very slight increase in wheelbase. Performance, however, was moderately improved over the Magnette Mark III, particularly in acceleration with zero to 60 mph now reached in 17 seconds. The maximum speed of 85 mph was scarcely affected. Fuel consumption was in the 22 to 25-miles-per-gallon range.

Though the Magnette ZA and ZB sold fairly well in the United States, the improved Marks III and IV, delivering at around $2,800, were caught in a deluge of American compact cars and submerged. It is a different story with the extremely popular M.G. 1100 which is as revolutionary as it is remarkable. Nothing quite like the M.G. 1100 is built by any other manufacturer.

Introduced in 1962, the 1100 "sports sedan" is a small 141-inch-overall car with exterior appearance and interior space that belie its modest circumstances. Employing unit-construction, the body is a full 60 inches wide allowing for two and sometimes three passengers in the rear seat. The front bucket seats and a flat floor accommodate 6-footers in surprising comfort. In other words, this small sedan is a family car with 9½ cubic feet of luggage space in the rear and parcel shelves beneath the dashboard and behind the rear seat.

Such generous space in so small a package would have been impossible in a conventional layout. Hence, M.G. placed the B.M.C. "A Series" engine crosswise in front where short shafts with universal joints drive the front wheels. The 1,098 cc. displacement engine is

Engine athwart and liquid suspension distinguish the M.G. 1100 sports sedan. (Joseph H. Wherry)

The 1,098 cc. engine of the Type 1100 sedan puts its port side forward. (Joseph H. Wherry)

tuned like the same unit in the Mark I Midget. Dual 1¼-inch S.U. carburetors and 8.9 to 1 compression ratio develop a modest 55 bhp at 5,500 rpm.

Weighing a mere 1,850 pounds ready at the curb, the 55 bhp available actually delivers more power to the driving wheels than would be obtained if a propeller shaft and rear wheel layout had been chosen.

The performance with two adults aboard is surprising. Through the gears to 60 mph takes a hair over 18 seconds and maximum speed is from 80 to 82 mph. Exceptionally economical to drive at relatively high cruising speeds over long distances, the 1100 will deliver upwards of 27 mpg under even adverse conditions and 30 mpg at a steady 60 mph.

Even more surprising is the quiet, smooth ride equaled by few cars at any price. The secret is the patented "Hydrolastic" four-wheel, independent suspension system. At the front are wishbones; trailing arms position the rear wheels.

There are no springs as such; rubber cones filled with a non-freezing water-based liquid at each wheel also take the place of shock absorbers. Anti-roll bars firmly resist undue heeling over on sharp corners. The liquid-filled rubber cones are sealed against leakage and front and rear units are inter-connected. When one wheel abruptly rises or drops, the displacing is immediately compensated for by corresponding leveling action at the other wheels.

In short, the Hydrolastic suspension system actually does what the highly touted air suspension was supposed to do but without mechanical complexity or fuss. Maintenance is virtually non-existent: M.G. suggests a pressure check of the suspension system after 12,000 miles. On the other hand, should road damage cause loss of fluid, rubber stops cushion the suspension members and one can safely drive any distance required at 30 mph.

The 1100 handles with the agility of a sports car. The driving position is comfortable but the steep angle of the steering column places the wheel at an angle which one has to accustom himself to. However, since rack-and-pinion steering is used, it is light, takes only three turns lock-to-lock, and needs less than 35 feet turning diameter. All this makes the 1100 one of the easiest cars to drive.

The fairly high performance for such a small family car is made even safer by 8-inch-diameter disc brakes in front. The rear brakes are 8-inch-drum types. Stopping distances at any given speed in the M.G. 1100 are less than in any standard American passenger car under the same conditions.

Two- and four-door sedans are available. Curved glass is used for all side windows; and very slender windshield and door pillars, and an unusually wide rear window, give unexcelled visibility. The M.G. motto of "Safety Fast" applies well to this model which was an immediate success. At well under $2,000 delivered anywhere in the U.S.A., the 1100 deserves its popularity.

So well has the 1100 model done that, as this is being written, it appears likely that a larger version, powered with the 1,798 cc. engine developing upwards of 90 horsepower, will come from M.G. on or before the first of 1967. This would, of course, replace the Magnette Mark IV in the larger family-car market, and be based on the already popular Austin 1800. With the more powerful engine driving the front wheels and with its ultra-soft but fine-handling suspension system, such a car would place M.G. in an enviable position. As things now stand, no American compact car for family

Space for four adults with baggage belie the 1100 sedan's small exterior. (Joseph H. Wherry)

use is expected to be able to compete with it in riding qualities, speed, and day-long cruising ability at a miserly fuel rate.

Clearly the most wanted model in the current line is the M.G.B. Replacing the M.G.A 1600 Mark II on the production line in the summer of 1962, the "B" is now in its fourth year and shows no indication of waning. Delivering at approximately $3,000 anywhere in the United States, the M.G.B is the top of the line and represents the final departure from separate frames and bodies.

As to styling, the M.G.B is a development of the M.G.A. Underneath the streamlined steel panels, however, the "B" is entirely different with body and frame combined into one integral, all welded, unit. The engine, although quite naturally benefiting from previous experience, is a completely new 1,798 cc. unit with five main bearings. This feature increases strength and overall durability. The overhead valves are pushrod-operated and the crankshaft is fully counterbalanced. Dual 1½-inch S.U. carburetors, aluminum alloy pistons, and 8.8 to 1 compression ratio are other features. The largest engine in any M.G. car since 1939, this very quiet powerplant turns out 98 bhp at 5,400 rpm and a torque of 107 to 110 foot-pounds in the 3,000 to 3,500 rpm range.

The 4-speed transmission is tougher, smoother, and has synchromesh on all but first gear. About 15% of the B's are sold with the excellent, electrically-controlled overdrive which is operated by the simple flick

The modern M.G.B contrasts interestingly with an old Spanish mission in California. (Joseph H. Wherry)

of a switch mounted on the dash to the left of the steering wheel. The overdrive functions in both top and third gears.

Principal dimensions underwent changes due to the completely new unit construction and engine. The wheelbase decreased a bit to 91 inches, the 153-inch length is 3 inches shorter, and the front tread is slightly increased to 49 inches. Bolted-on disc wheels are standard. Refinements, not changes, in the wishbones and coil springs were made in the independent front suspension. The rear axle is still rigid and controlled by semi-elliptic leaf springs. The propeller shaft is open. Hydraulic shock absorbers are used all around.

The brake system employs $10\frac{3}{4}$-inch discs in front and 10-inch-diameter drums in the rear, all by Lockheed. M.G. enthusiasts, a particular lot not generally happy with change for its own sake, were delighted that rack-and-pinion steering with three turns lock-to-lock was retained.

Still the most widely owned of all true sports cars, the M.G. in its current "B" series has won its share of honors in racing. The most recent victory was the Class GT-9 first place at Sebring in March, 1966. The International Grand Tourismo Class allows only very minor engine modifications. Probably more impressive than the class win is that the M.G.B took third place overall for Grand Tourismo cars.

For the sports car driver, performance is a criterion, particularly in such an old and distinguished marque. Running a fairly stiff M.G.B with only some 4,000 miles

A prototype M.G.B at Le Mans in 1965 displays some unusual lines. (British Motor Corp.)

The M.G.B winning its GT-9 class at Sebring in March, 1966. (British Motor Corp.)

showing on the odometer, the author achieved the following performance figures:

>Acceleration 0 to 30 mph: 3.1 seconds
>Acceleration 0 to 45 mph: 5.9 seconds
>Acceleration 0 to 60 mph: 11.1 seconds

>Speed in 1st gear: 31 mph
>Speed in 2nd gear: 48 mph
>Speed in 3rd gear: 76 mph
>Speed in 4th gear: 105 mph

The gear speeds are without overdrive in operation, of course. As for maximum speed, the factory states that the M.G.B will top out in direct fourth gear at 107 mph. The author believes it will; he simply ran out of space in both directions and a bit of speed was still left. With overdrive actuated, a little more speed could be attained. The factory lists speed in fourth gear per 1,000 rpm at 17.9 mph; in overdrive, 22.3 mph per 1,000 rpm is attained.

The car tested weighed 2,138 pounds in two-seater form, neither very light nor very heavy. Overall fuel consumption checked out at 26.6 miles per gallon including acceleration and high speed runs. Normal driving using overdrive, which does not disengage the clutch when below overdrive range, brings fuel consumption down to 28 to 30 miles per gallon. Consequently, the M.G.B rates as a very economical car, especially in view of the relatively high potential performance. The brake system is more than adequate to cope with the performance available in the hands of a competent driver, and handling and roadability are excellent.

Creature comforts include individual seats, upholstered in genuine leather, with adjustable backrests. Behind the seats is space for luggage or a youngster or two if very young. The luggage boot holds the spare wheel and will accommodate several suitcases of moderate size. Full carpeting with rubber mats on the floor and into the scuttle adds a luxury note. No longer is polished wood used on the dashboard, or facia, but a full complement of instruments including a tachometer remains. The parking brake is not of the fly-off type but its location between the seats is convenient. Perhaps the most appreciated improvement over its forerunner is the wind-up windows making the M.G.B a true all-weather vehicle. Among the many B.M.C. options are radios, knock-off wire wheels, and air-conditioning.

Very late in 1965, the works introduced a beautifully streamlined model officially named the M.G.B-GT, a *grand tourismo*. An additional bench seat provides more comfortable occasional seating making the "GT" a family sports car in the grand tradition. When the backrest of this rear seat is folded flat, a remarkable amount of luggage can be carried. Full, thick carpeting covers this compartment and the rear side windows are hinged to open, facilitating ventilation. At about $3,100 delivered in the U.S.A., the "GT" is a prestige car in an economy package reflecting traditional British automotive craftsmanship.

The specifications of the "GT" are synonymous with those of the M.G.B two-seater. Though weighing about 50 pounds more, the GT's better streamlining should net an additional two or three miles an hour.

When the Midget Mark I in its 1,098 cc. form was

Wind-up windows and other creature comforts make the M.G.B a dual-purpose car. (Joseph H. Wherry)

Two-plus-two seating is the contribution of the M.G.B-GT to one-car families with a flair for the best of both car worlds. (Joseph H. Wherry)

The space behind the cockpit in the M.G.B-GT is spacious. (Joseph H. Wherry)

The M.G.B-GT is a natural development in the grand tradition. The young lady agrees. (Joseph H. Wherry)

The Midget Mark II is improved with wind-up windows and 90-miles-per-hour performance. (Joseph H. Wherry)

The Midget Mark II is powered by a 1,098 cc. engine. (Joseph H. Wherry)

phased out in 1964, its place was taken by the Mark II. Still in production, the Mark II looks the same at a distance. Examined closely, the changes are apparent: roll-up windows in the doors which now have external keyway locks, swiveling side-window vents, and a redesigned panel which still contains the usual instruments.

Engine changes include a 9.0 to 1 compression ratio and timing refined to produce 59 bhp at 5,750 rpm. This represents the present high point of development for the 1,098 cc., "A Series," 3-main-bearing engine, which is shared with the 1100 sports sedan, the latter in decreased tune as we have seen. The torque developed is 62 foot-pounds at 3,250 rpm.

Suspension changes are also few but the substitution of full semi-elliptic rear leaf springs for the quarter-elliptics used in the Mark I Midget improves handling and resistance to rear-end bounce. As on its big brother, Lockheed brakes are used, 8¼-inch discs in front and 7-inch drums in the rear. Rack-and-pinion steering, with but two and one-third turns lock-to-lock, give the same quick handling with cornering qualities improved by refined front spring rates.

The author had not driven a Midget since the 948 cc. Mark I was replaced. Hence, the following performance figures were most enlightening and just a bit exciting,

Instrument location in the Midget Mark II is complete and functional. (Joseph H. Wherry)

considering that just 1,098 cc. of engine moves a car which weighs 1,572 pounds at the curb:

Acceleration 0 to 30 mph: 4.2 seconds
Acceleration 0 to 45 mph: 9.3 seconds
Acceleration 0 to 60 mph: 14.8 seconds

Speed in 1st gear: 31 mph
Speed in 2nd gear: 50 mph
Speed in 3rd gear: 69 mph
Speed in 4th gear: 93 mph

Fuel consumption of 27 miles per gallon in average city and country driving increases to 30 mpg, or more, on highways with a steady throttle foot at 60–65 mph. With a fuel tank holding 7¼ gallons, one can count on from 180 to 200 miles between refills.

Most Mark II Midgets are imported with wire wheels and deliver for around $2,150 without the optional radio or detachable hardtop. With the wind-up windows, the Mark II is a true convertible. Evidently the roadster days are gone forever. If one insists, a Midget with the listed disc wheels as standard could probably be purchased.

In any event, the Midget Mark II is by no means the least or the last. It was followed by the Mark III which was introduced in October, 1966, at the London Auto Show. It differs from the Mark II principally in having a re-designed "quick-lift" top and a B.M.C. 1,275 cc. engine instead of the 1,098 cc. unit.

What's in the Midget's future? Prototypes of the related Sprite have been seen powered with 1,293 cc.

Popularity of the M.G. Midget Mark II assures a successful fourth decade for the Midget tribe. (Joseph H. Wherry)

engines. This could mean a future 105-mph Midget, a worthy successor to a tribe with bloodlines going back over four decades.

SPECIFICATIONS

Type and Name	Cylinders	Bore and Stroke (mm.)	Displacement (cc.)	Compression Ratio ($1/m$ to 1)	Brake Horsepower @ rpm	Transmission Speeds	Gear Ratios	Rear Axle Ratios	Tires	Wheelbase (inches)	Tread, Front and Rear (inches)
Magnette Mark III	4	73 x 88.9	1,489	8.3	68 @ 5,500	4	1.00 1.37 2.21 3.64	4.55	14 x 5.60	99 3/16	48 7/8 49 7/8
Magnette Mark IV	4	76.2 x 88.9	1,622	8.3	71 @ 5,000	4	1.00 1.37 2.21 3.64	4.3 Front drive	14 x 5.60	100 1/2	50 5/8 51 3/8
1100	4	64.6 x 83.7	1,098	8.9	55 @ 5,500	4	1.00 1.41 2.17 3.63	4.13	12 x 5.20	93 1/2	51 1/2 50 5/8
B (incl.: M.G.B.-GT)	4	80.3 x 88.9	1,798	8.8	98 @ 5,400	4	1.00 1.37 2.21 3.63 0.85 1.10 with o'dr.	3.91	14 x 5.60	91	49 49 1/4
Midget Mark II	4	64.6 x 83.7	1,098	9.0	59 @ 5,750	4	1.00 1.357 1.916 3.20	4.22	13 x 5.20	80	45 3/4 44 3/4

JOSEPH H. WHERRY

was born in 1918 in Everett, Washington, and now lives with his wife, Bettye, and their four children in Santa Rosa, California. He is the author of many general and special interest magazine articles and ten books, and when "time permits, which it seldom does," likes to build airplane and railroad models to scale. A photographer as well as a writer, Mr. Wherry illustrates many of his own works. He has contributed to *Motor Trend* and *Road and Track* magazines, and from 1956 to 1958 was the Detroit editor of *Motor Trend*. With his interest in things automotive, it was natural for him to turn his skills to books on the subject. Among his published titles in this field are *Economy Car Blitz, Antique and Classic Cars,* and *The MG Story*. The last and *The Jaguar Story* by Mr. Wherry, which is now in preparation, are books in Chilton's Sebring Series. *Automobiles of the World* is also in preparation.